4.95

CHARLES DE FOUCAULD

D1528471

Charles de Foucauld

THE SILENT WITNESS

by

SERGIUS C. LORIT

K-P
new city press, new york

New City Press

206 Skillman Avenue

Brooklyn, N.Y. 11211

Original edition: *Charles de Foucauld, Il Deserto che Chiama*
©Citta' Nuova Editrice, Rome 1966

Translated from the Italian by Ted Morrow
©1977 New City Press of the Focolare Movement, Inc.

Third Printing 1983
ISBN 0-911782-29-X

Contents

Scion of the House of Foucauld

At five o'clock on a June morning in Algiers, daylight has already arrived — even in the *mellah,* the Jewish ghetto, where the shadows of a dying night cling longest among the dirty, dilapidated huts leaning against one another for support. The sky stretches brightly overhead, and the women are already busy indoors, however empty and silent the streets outside remain. Footsteps, at an hour like this, fling sonorous echoes against the walls, and the echoes call curious eyes to the windows.

Naturally the unusual 5 A.M. visit of June 10, 1883, did not go unobserved. A young stranger, of medium build and dressed in the nattiest European style, was seen calling at the mud-stained shanty of Rabbi Mardochee ben Abi Seror, who lived there with his aging wife and four sons.

This mysterious happening in the *mellah* was a topic of conversation for quite some time, because — according to the testimony of a hundred self-

appointed detectives covering the case behind
closed doors — the European never came out again.
What actually emerged about an hour later was
another stranger, this one decked out in a half-
Algerian, half-Syrian costume — a red skullcap and
black silk turban on his head, a dark-colored
Turkish *yelek* over a loose-sleeved white shirt,
and knee-length breeches. He paused a moment in
the doorway to don a cowled woolen robe; then,
accompanied by Mardochee, he quickly left the
ghetto. Someone heard Mardochee call him " Joseph
Aleman "; someone said he heard him use the term
" rabbi. "

It was several years before the secret came out:
that this " Rabbi Joseph Aleman " was the same
young man who had come to Mardochee's house
at dawn, only now in disguise. He was none other
than Viscount Charles de Foucauld, whose extraordinarily prodigal and shocking way of life had
provoked so much gossip in Saumur, Pont-à-
Mousson, and Paris, not to mention the violent
feelings and contemptuous jokes he inspired among
the French troops stationed in Algeria.

Charles de Foucauld was born at Strasbourg
twenty-five years before the above incident occurred
— on September 15, 1858, to be exact. Napoleon
III reigned as French emperor, and the newspaper
business in those days was brisk, thanks to the
apparitions at Lourdes.

At No. 9, Place de Broglie, where he was born, the very stones cried out in a declaration of the occupants' wealth, aristocracy, and ancestral glory. The furniture, the pictures, the knick-knacks, curtains, and upholstery — all seemed by design and construction the appropriate field for an ancient coat-of-arms hanging at the end of an imposing hallway — a roaring red lion astride a shiny bridge between arches argent, holding aloft the militant motto, *Jamais arrière* (Never retreat), of the Viscounts of Pontbriand.

Bertrand de Foucauld, in fact, never retreated during the Seventh Crusade, and fell as one of the heroes at Mansurah as he rode with King St. Louis. Jean de Foucauld was no slacker either, for the family records tell us he stood beside Joan of Arc in the nave of Rheims Cathedral during Charles VII's coronation ceremonies. Then there was Armand de Foucauld, better known as Jean-Marie du Lau, Archbishop of Arles. He did not cringe in fear when the French Revolution came, but died a martyr at Paris, in the Carmelites' prison, during the September 1792 massacre. (Pius XI beatified him in 1926.) Even Edouard de Foucauld, Charles' father, a third-generation public servant, was not one to shrink from his duties as inspector of streams and forests.

Charles' mother, Elizabeth de Morlet, was likewise descended from an illustrious military family, but no one could care less about this than she. A deeply committed Christian, she had Charles baptized when he was two days old. When he was three, his sister Marie joined the family, and from a very early age the mother brought them up in the law of God, above all teaching them to pray and to look after the poor.

We must admit that all this maternal, religious instruction aroused little enthusiasm in young Charles, at least from what evidence we have of his childhood, which never indicates the slightest inclination toward any kind of piety — let alone a religious vocation. Nevertheless, if the lessons he received in the Christian life seemed fruitless at the time, they were so strongly impressed upon his youthful soul that he was to discover them three years afterward, fresh and powerful enough to convince us he must never have forgotten them.

In 1863, when Charles had just turned five years old and the summer was at its height, the shadow of the cross fell over the noble household of Foucauld de Pontbriand. Edouard, Charles' father, contracted tuberculosis, and his health went downhill rapidly; he had to give up his official duties, and from that day onward his morale kept sinking lower and lower. He withdrew into a tortured, touchy silence, as though possessed of some demon. One day he deserted his children and his wife (who was expecting a third child) and fled to his sister Inés — one of the famous beauties of that era. (She had, in fact, served as a model for the painter Ingres.)

Elizabeth, meanwhile, fled the splendor of her home on Place de Broglie, betaking herself and her two children to the Rue des Eschasses and the home of her father M. de Morlet, a retired artillery colonel and a very charming personality. The following March, however, she passed away — from complications in childbirth, but perhaps also with a broken heart. Her last words were the ones uttered at Gethsemane: " Father, not my will, but thine be done. " Five months later, at Inés' home, Edouard also breathed his last, leaving Charles and Marie complete orphans.

So it was that the colonel, their grandfather, already past his 77th birthday, took over complete responsibility for them. He practically worshiped Charles: " When he cries — he said — I see my little girl all over again. " And Charles repaid him with a profound affection.

When the boy was eight he entered the St. Arbogast diocesan school in Strasbourg, where he remained until it was time to go to the lycèe — the public high school.

He was an average student. All his teachers seem to agree that he was an unusually bright boy, but more than one was annoyed by his generally indifferent behavior.

War came in 1870, when the Germans attacked France's eastern border. M. de Morlet saw the trouble brewing and, lacking confidence in Napoleon III's ability to cope with it, fled with his grandchildren to Switzerland. And just in time, because the German cannons soon forced Strasbourg to surrender. Napoleon was defeated at Sedan, and France declared herself a republic once more. Paris, besieged, surrendered to escape utter starvation; and Alsace-Lorraine became German territory.

M. de Morlet, ex-colonel of the French Army's artillery, had seen enough of Strasbourg, and now preferred to establish himself in Nancy, taking up residence on the Rue du Manège. At Nancy, Charles attended his third high school. In 1872, at the age of fourteen and already a fully-grown young man, he received first Communion and Confirmation.

At that time he experienced a great illumination of soul, but it was soon to sputter out. Once enrolled in high school, he fell in love with the sceptics of every age of history, from Horace to Montaigne, with a special preference for the classical comic dramatist Aristophanes. Unbelief was much in vogue among the middle classes in those days, and the working class had its prophets of atheism. The voices of Berthelot, Renan, Taine, Anatole-France, Nietzsche, Marx, and Rimbaud were heard everywhere, sounding their battle cries against religion. Charles had never read a single line by these authors, but his spirit responded to the breezes set in motion by their ideas, and that was enough to make him jettison his faith. " For twelve years, " he was to write later, " I lived without a faith; nothing actually seemed to have any certainty about it. The very credulity with which the world pursued a thousand different

12

religions seemed a good enough argument for me to renounce them all."

When he graduated from the lycèe in 1874, the moment had arrived for Charles to seek his fortune in the outside world. He went to Paris to study philosophy.

M. de Morlet had arranged for his matriculation in a Jesuit boarding school on the Rue des Postes, but the young man found the place unbearable. He implored and begged and wheedled his grandpapà, in letters by the dozen, to come and take him back to Nancy. But the old man held out against his pleas, and by New Year's, in spite of everything, Charles had his Bachelor of Philosophy.

Now Charles de Foucauld de Pontbriand must decide how he would earn a living, although for him there was really no " choice. " From the day of his birth it had seemed quite obvious to everyone that a man of his family legacy would follow a military career; and Charles had always assumed that this was the natural, logical thing to do.

Grandfather Morlet would have preferred enrolling his young charge in the École Polytechnique, preparatory to becoming an artillery officer. But Charles regarded engineering as too much of a " grind " for him, and he had no taste whatsoever for this sort of thing. He wouldn't mind becoming an officer, but not the hard-working kind. St. Cyr Military School was the place for him; and besides, it was easier to get in.

But St. Cyr's prerequisite was a year of prep

school in Paris, and Paris meant another brush with the Jesuits at a boarding school. It was a year of new troubles for the aging M. de Morlet, for every two days the postman arrived with a letter from his grandson. These were desperate letters, sometimes 40 pages long, declaring that the situation was absolutely hopeless and that the writer must return home at once.

At years's end he did come home, expelled on grounds of laziness and lack of discipline. Later he was to write, in describing this period of his life, " I was so completely selfish, so completely vain, so completely irreligious, and utterly given over to wickedness, that I was only one step from insanity! "

Grandpa did not rest content with Charles' expulsion, but turned him over to competent tutors, urging him to go ahead and take the entrance exams for St. Cyr.

Charles was nearly disqualified from taking the exams for being overweight. At 18 he was 5',9½ " and terribly fat and flabby, from an overindulgence in sweets, fancy meats, rare wines, and comfortable chairs. But finally the board of examiners decided that a couple of months at St. Cyr would take off some of the excess pounds, and let him take the tests. He ranked 82nd among 412 candidates. Two years later he would stand 333rd among 386. And to think that he began with so much enthusiasm!

Now that he was at St. Cyr he was truly " a man " and truly " free! " And the " free man, " to his credit, docilely accepted military discipline for a few months, though often slow to catch on to it. He was proud to wear the famous red and white feather in the equally famous *kepi* — cap — worn at this school. But then he became cronies with the Marquis de Morès, a reckless playboy, and after that his studies, his discipline, and his duties went into eclipse. In two years he accumulated forty-five punishments for neglect of duty, irresponsibility, and nonconformity to discipline. That he passed his exams at all was due to his keen intelligence and retentive memory.

Meanwhile grandfather Morlet died, and this was a great loss to him. But on September 15, 1878, his twentieth birthday, he inherited the family fortune, which turned out to be considerable. It had an intoxicating effect on young Charles de Foucauld, because for him it was a golden key, opening the way to success.

He decided to become a cavalry officer; the Marquis de Morès had the same inspiration. Did they get through St. Cyr by the skin of their teeth? Well then, at Cavalry School in Saumur they would squeeze through the keyhole!

At Saumur they roomed together in No. 82. Morès kept them both in clothes and shoes — all in the latest style. Foucauld concentrated on making things comfortable and epicurean: sumptuous snacks and a ravishing easy chair — plus a divan as a standby.

" If you have not seen Foucauld in his room, clad in his white flannel pajamas buttoned with frogs, sprawled leisurely on his divan or in a commodious armchair, enjoying a tasty liverwurst sandwich, washing it down with a high-grade champagne, reading a luxuriously bound edition of Aristophanes, then you have never seen a man really enjoying himself." So reads the account of a friend, written at the time. And another makes the comment: " The room these two live in has become famous overnight for its delicious snacks and protracted card parties for the benefit of one of them who was being punished — because it was quite a rare occasion when one of them was not being confined to quarters for some reason."

In a nutshell, Charles had a record of 21 days of " open " confinement and 45 of strict confinement, and Morès fared no better. Whenever they could leave the base, they would entice a gay company of followers over to Budan's, Saumur's most beloved and celebrated restaurant. There, in a private room, they would order the most exquisite of meals. Charles preferred cold partridge pie, served with two bottles of Alicante. Afterward, stretched out on a sofa, he would philosophize, saying that " after a meal there was nothing quite like a good cigar. " Then he would go home in a cab, choosing one as small and low as possible, so that he would not have " the agony of stepping too high to enter it. " And as an aftermath to each of these " banquets," the gossip mills of Saumur would be grinding for days on end.

But all this was child's play to the Viscount of Pontbriand. To supplement these " normal " orgies there were some extraordinary adventures added for spice. One day when he was, as usual, under strict confinement, he learned of a ball being held at Tours. He acquired a worker's cap and coveralls and a false beard, and clad in these he left the camp without any trouble from the guards. When the train stopped at Tours, he decided to have a little snack before going to the ball. The owner of the restaurant was at once suspicious, because his weird customer's little goatee was beginning to come unglued! Was he a gangster or a revolutionary? At any rate, it wouldn't hurt to call the police.

At the police station Charles explained his little escapade so capably that the commissioner let him go with nothing but a big slap on the back. In fact, the poor fellow was in tears from having laughed so much. But just after Charles left police headquarters, whom should he meet but General L'Hotte, commanding officer of Saumur School. You guessed it! He got 30 days more of strict confinement.

In October, 1879, Charles de Foucauld finished 86th in a class of 87 at the Cavalry School. The Inspector General made the following comments on him: " He is a remarkable person and has received a good education. But he has a big head, and he has no thought for anything except entertainment. His furlough has been canceled on grounds of bad conduct and his record of frequent punishments. "

He was commissioned a second lieutenant of the Fourth Regiment of Hussars at Sézanne. But

Sézanne did not offer him enough diversions, and so he transferred to Pont-à-Mousson, where his first act was to rent an apartment. He rented another in Paris, to have handy when he decided to spend a furlough in the capital.

He had grown fatter than ever by now (the St. Cyr " weight reduction program " had been a perfect flop.) His face looked swollen, he had the lips of one who hankers after rare gourmands, the devilish expression of one who lives a fast life, the pomaded hair-do of a gigolo. " He was one fellow who really lived it up, " comments Duc de FitzJames, who often served as Morès' stand-in on the Foucauld expeditions; Morès had become a mounted policeman. " Foucauld always shared what he had with us, and always observed the greatest delicacy and finesse in doing so. If we were playing for money, and he saw that he was winning too much, I have seen him deliberately throw the game. He found great delight in treating first one small group, then another. Often he invited us to his attractive *garçonnière* to enjoy liverwurst washed down with the finest of cherry brandy. He kept a servant, an English bicycle, and a horse. "

During this time Charles became acquainted with a certain Mimi; he had been keeping her about a year when (December 1880) he received notice that the Fourth Hussars were being transferred to Algeria to man the garrison of Sétif, where they would be known as the Fourth African Rifle Regiment. Charles, who could not bear being separated from Mimi, hatched a new piece of mischief. He gave her a letter of introduction and had her leave for Algeria two days ahead of the regiment. Mimi presented herself at the seaport of Bone, and again at Sétif, as Mrs. Charles de Foucauld, Viscountess of Pontbriand (as was stated in the letter) and the military authorities extended her every courtesy possible. But when the colonel and the other regimental officers arrived with their legitimate wives, the cat was out of the bag.

The colonel heaped abuse on his scandalous second lieutenant, but the lieutenant couldn't care less. If anything, the rebuke only provoked him to a greater public display of his affection for Mimi, bringing such a storm of protest that the colonel finally gave him an ultimatum: " Either Mimi or the regiment. Take your choice. " Charles defiantly replied that he would not think of sending Mimi back to France.

And so, on March 20, 1881, a federal order placed Lieutenant Charles de Foucauld on inactive duty " for actions unbefitting his rank, for breach of discipline, and for unbecoming conduct in public. "

Charles' career was finished, but he celebrated it with a peal of laughter, took Mimi by the arm, and led her to Evian, Switzerland, to live.

But one day three months later, as he was by chance glancing through a newspaper, he read that in Algeria the sheik, Uled Sidi, had risen in revolt, and that the Fourth African Infantry was engaged with them in full combat. *Jamais arrière!* And at that moment Mimi lost all her attraction for him.

Flying to Paris, he swooped down on the Minister of War, asking to be readmitted to the army immediately. And when they hesitated, still remembering his scandalous record, he assured them that he cared nothing about his rank — whatever he might have been entitled to as yet — but was ready to go as an enlisted man. He was readmitted as an officer, took the first boat to Africa, and was soon in the midst of all the excitement.

No one would have recognized him any more. This was an entirely new person, even if his pocket edition of Aristophanes still went with him everywhere.

" Amidst the dangers and discomforts that accompanied most of this campaign, " writes a comrade in arms, " this educated dilettante showed himself a soldier and officer capable of undergoing the severest trials with a smile on his face always ready to take responsibility, and occupied, above all, with a loving concern for his men. "

He fought to win, for he believed without question that Uled Sidi Sheik must be destroyed. Yet at the same time he was deeply impressed by the heavily hooded Arabs who bowed so solemnly in prayer, and their lofty invocation, *Allah' u akbar* (God is greater).

"At the age of 16, with a book-taught faith," writes the biographer Michel Carrouges, "he had concluded that the differences between religions were the best reason for discounting them all. But here at the edge of the desert he saw the believers in Islam at prayer, and was seized with feelings of envy and admiration." Foucauld himself would confess, in time, that "Islam was responsible for a profound change within me . . . . My exposure to this faith, and to these souls living always in God's presence, helped me to understand that there is something greater and more real than the pleasures of the world."

God, in other words, had used the faith of the followers of Mohammed to make his first breakthrough to the soul of Charles de Foucauld.

When hostilities ceased, and the Fourth Infantry returned to Sétif, Charles felt that he could not dissociate himself from this newly discovered world. He asked for a leave of absence to make a study tour of southern Algeria. He was refused. And so, for the second time, he left the army, and this time for something more meaningful than Mimi.

He went to Algiers and took up residence at No. 58 Ramp de Vallee. Was he refused a study tour in the Algerian interior? Very well, then! He would explore Morocco. Yes, Morocco the impenetrable, the Moslems' Atlantic stronghold, with its storied cities, its colorful bazaars, its labyrinthine streets shrouded in mystery, its hidden gardens. This was the domain of Moulay el Hasan, the all-powerful Sultan, and the home of perpetual anarchy, the country that hermetically sealed off its ports to Europeans, because in every European it saw not only an obvious infidel but a secret spy.

But a meticulous preparation was necessary. All Charles' laziness and shallowness disappeared as though by magic, and he began a siege of the Algiers library, studying Arabic and the geography and ethnography of Morocco, reading and tracing of maps, studying the use of scientific apparatus. And the head librarian, Oscar MacCarthy, proved himself of inestimable help to Charles in his work.

Then, while he was so engrossed in his studies, he received a sudden, unexpected blow. His aunt Inés, no longer the beautiful aunt Inés to whom his father had fled when dying, accused him of squandering an enormous sum of money (four thousand francs a month for a period of four years!). She had obtained a court order at Nancy to have her prodigal young nephew placed under a legal guardian.

Charles did not deny that he had done some terrible things; that he had, to say the least, made very extravagant use of his money; but now things were different.

All the court cared about was his admission of guilt. He was declared " prodigal " and a financial guardian was assigned him, who turned out to be an older cousin, M. de Lateuche of Nancy. M. de Lateuche put Charles on a monthly allowance of 350 francs — just when his large fortune would have enabled him to do something really worthwhile! Charles was also allowed a supplementary payment, but only if it went toward the purchase of a sextant, a chronometer, a theodolite, and some other equipment necessary for the expedition.

Charles again threw himself into his studies. Duc de FitzJames, his fellow playboy in the days of Pont-à-Mousson, ran across him one day. " How my old buddy Foucauld has changed, " he wrote to some friends. " He used to be such a butterball and now he is quite skinny. He has had enough of parties and women and fancy foods. Now all he does is study! "

Meanwhile, as Charles practiced using his scientific equipment — aboard a naval vessel moored at Algiers and commanded by one of his relatives — M. MacCarthy was looking for someone who would make a good guide for the expedition. He felt he had found his man, the day he ran into Rabbi Mardochee ben Abi Seror, whose adventurous life already read like a storybook. Negotiations with the aging Hebrew took a long time and a lot of work; every time they met to discuss the trip, the old rascal would raise the price of his services. But in the end he agreed upon 270 francs a month for the six to seven months the safari was supposed to last. In those days, it was very good wages.

On the morning when our story opened, June 10, 1883, it was these two men, Mardochee and

Foucauld, whom we met leaving the Jewish ghetto of Algiers, at the very beginning of their journey. As a European, Charles could not have set foot inside Morocco. To disguise himself as an Arab would have been foolish also; the gaps in his knowledge of the Arabic language and the Islamic religion would have been too easily detected. So he was masquerading as a Jew. With the help of Mardochee, this 25-year-old " rabbi, " alias Joseph Aleman, would find asylum and protection among Jews in all the forbidden cities of Morocco.

The Wandering Rabbi

On April 25, 1885, Paris newspapers gave front-page coverage to a story concerning a special session of the Geographical Society, whose President was Ferdinand de Lesseps, famed builder of the Suez Canal. On the previous day the Society had listened to an account of the expedition to Morocco by 25-year-old Viscount Charles de Foucauld de Pontbriand, upon whom they had already conferred a gold medal.

"Before M. Foucauld came along" said the French and foreign papers that day, "a mere 12, 208 kilometers of Morocco were known to map-makers, the latitudinal reference points were few and inaccurate, and the longitudes were even more vague. Within the whole sultanate, only about twenty localites had actually been logged with astronomical instruments . . . . In nine months, between June 28, 1883, and March 23, 1884, one man, the Viscount Charles de Foucauld, has more than doubled the distance in Morocco traveled thus far by explorers, and has given accurate descriptions of his trip. He has retraced 689 kilometers covered by his predecessors, in some cases correcting their observatons, and has explored 2,250 kilometers of new territory. With instruments he has logged 45 longitudes and 40 latitudes, and whereas before we possessed only a few dozen altitude readings, he has recorded about 3,000. Thanks to the Viscount de Foucauld we have begun a truly new era in Moroccan geography. "

This chapter in the life of Charles de Foucauld is a story all its own. The report of the Geographical Society is only concerned with its unusual significance for science, but for Charles this was also a time of rupture with the past, by means of a responsible, daring act that he performed with great punctilio, avenging himself on the dissipations of a once unprofitable existence. So we will want to give some attention to this part of his life.

The young viscount and his elderly guide first tried to penetrate Morocco via the rugged Riff Mountains that border on Algeria, but this was not successful.

They were quite a pair, these two travelers. Charles de Foucauld, alias Joseph Aleman, presented himself as a Muscovite rabbi who had fled Russia during the latest pogroms. In his half-Syrian, half-Algerian costume, he bore a grotesque similarity to one of those brightly costumed monkeys that perform little stunts on their owners' shoulders.

Mardochee ben Abi Seror, on the other hand, was a real rabbi and an experienced traveler, although now only a shadow of his former adventurous self. His long black beard was by now spotted and streaked with gray. His caftan, gathered tightly at the waist, hung all the way to his feet, and he wore a red skull cap and black turban. The original expensiveness of his clothing was almost unrecognizable amid the stains and patches. Now a timid, decrepit old man, Mardochee was also afflicted with near-blindness and near-deafness. His constant companion was a snuffbox, which he used continually, and his favorite topic of conversation with anyone and everyone was alchemy, for he was an avid searcher for " the philosopher's stone, " that legendary object that was supposed to convert other metals into gold. This was the guide to whom Charles de Foucauld entrusted himself on one of the most difficult and dangerous expeditions of that era.

They wasted about ten days in Oran, Tlemcen, Lalla-Marnia, and Nemours, searching the alleys and synagogues for some Jew who might help them get past the border into the occult empire of Sultan Moulay Hasan.

Wearing his white *barrakan* and a veil over his face, the tall, majestic Sultan rode a white charger covered with a gold-bordered green caparison. Around him swarmed a cloud of slaves, struggling to keep the flies away and to shade him from the sun with a giant red parasol. A vast retinue of

27

dignitaries attended him: the standard-bearers, the guards with their ostentatious red uniforms, the musicians perpetually serenading him — all of this great assembly constantly in motion across his vast empire, a domain without streets or bridges, eroded with hunger and riddled with violence. From capital to capital he rode — from Fez to Rabat, from Meknès to Marakesh — or else to one of his distant " protectorates " to exact tribute by force of arms or to quell a tribal rebellion. And when evening fell, around his own gold-studded tent there blossomed a whole canvas city, spreading outward in concentric circles and divided into separate living quarters for the officials, the harem, the guards and merchants, his native soldiery, and warriors conscripted from conquered tribes.

This was Morocco as those outside Morocco know it, their information pieced together from the reports of those few who had ventured inside its borders and returned alive to tell about it. It was a country savagely inhospitable to strangers, and fanatically resistant to anything " Christian. " Not only did its rigorous legal system exact the death penalty for spying, but there was also a state of constant political unrest that tended to brutalize everyone and everything to be found within its borders.

Only one city, Tangier, was open to Europeans, a place where Morocco could do business with the rest of the world. Here Europeans lived with a relative degree of security. Charles de Foucauld and his guide, having failed in every attempt to enter Morocco overland, took to the sea and landed in Tangier.

It was June 20, 1883, when they saw the great port basking in the sun, its white houses interspersed among the olive trees, its lofty palm trees and its spiked minarets piercing the blue of the skies to produce a brilliant, multicolored mosaic. Charles became submerged in the cosmopolitan crowds, where he rubbed shoulders with Europeans, Jews, Arabs, Berbers, and Negro slaves. His wanderings took him through a maze of narrow, winding streets. He heard the cries of the street hawkers; the hoofbeats of the horses, their riders swathed heavily in Arab *burnouses;* the eerie intonations of the snake charmers; the tinkling of bells that announced the water peddlers and the staccato plop-plops made by the hoofs of their donkeys, bearing goatskin containers; the sorrowful complaints of beggars and the insistent cries of charlatans; the rhythmic incantations of singers and musicians — all but drowning out the calls of black-veiled venders, squatting next to their meager little piles of merchandise: dates, poultry, vegetables, and pottery. Charles finally found where the French Minister resided and later he made his way to the home of Moulay Abd es Selam, descendant of Mohammed and a friend of France. Both these personages furnished him with letters of introduction to people who might sometime prove useful to him.

Chapter One in the Moroccan sojourn went off very well indeed. They rented some mules and loaded them up with the necessary supplies: a blanket and a change of clothes for each of them, a few items of food, cooking utensils, a medicine kit with first aid supplies, and a metal box containing the secret equipment necessary for exploration — sextant, theodolite, chronometer, some compasses and thermometers, barometers and topographical maps. Three thousand francs in gold and coral — the expedition's working funds — were sewed inside Charles' tunic in a pocket unknown even to Mardochee. Then they each mounted a mule and headed for whatever unknown fate awaited them a Tetuán.

On the way there, Charles had a little discussion with his guide: " Listen carefully, Mardochee. When you were trying a few days ago to convince one after another of your co-religionists to help us get into the Riff, I didn't say much, but I was getting really worried. You always think up such fantastic stories about my exotic Russian origins. You invent too many tales about me, and you make them too fantastic. Your mania for spinning yarns could lead you to saying more than you should, and then you know what would happen to us! So let's simplify the whole affair. From now on, I'm not Rabbi Joseph Aleman escaped from Moscow, etc., but just plain Rabbi Couvaud, originally from Jerusalem. Period. Do you understand? "

So they arrived in Tetuán without any incidents.

Could it be that the real Morocco wasn't as bad as reported?

Feeling elated over what had happened so far, and finding very warm hospitality with a family in the ghetto, they launched at once into preparation for Round Two, which would be a more ambitious undertaking — an expedition to Sheshauen, the Arabs' holy city, a place no European had ever seen.

They left in high spirits but just a few hours later the people in the Tetuán ghetto saw them returning in haste, their faces very pale and their clothes torn. Just outside the city some Arabs who had been watching the scientific instruments that " Rabbi Couvaud " was using and who suspected him of espionage, made a headlong rush at him with assassination as their object. " It's a miracle we're still alive, " stammered Mardochee, who had by now completely lost all his nerve of younger days.

Charles realized at once that this was his first brush with the real Morocco. It would thus behoove him, if he were going to study the geography of the country and its other characteristics, to give priority to studying the local situation, to get a knowledge in depth of the Moors' way of life and their own methods of getting things done. After gathering his data, he sized up the situation as follows: the country swarmed with predatory creatures who exacted tribute mercilessly from the people who cultivated the land. They snatched away whatever crumbs might have escaped after the Sultan and his greedy, pompous court had licked the tax platter clean.

As regards the practical realities of traveling through these domains, Foucauld hit upon the following three-step procedure: 1) ask a responsible person of the tribe presently entertaining him to give him his *anäia* (protection); 2) add to this the *zettet,* a sum of money paid for such protection; 3) travel to the destination specified in the company of the person from whom he was buying protection, and attended by heavily armed men. After traveling to the next point in the custody of friends, he would then make a new contract, again requesting *anäia,* paying new *zettet,* and proceeding with an armed escort — always hoping he would not run into some band of marauders more powerful than his escort. This is how he conducted the rest of his voyage across Morocco.

Having learned his lesson, Charles immediately applied it to the problem of getting to Fez. All along the way, under the constant menace of bandits and the suspicious gaze of his fellow travelers, he managed secretly to make his first observations with compass and barometer, beginning the clandestine routine of note-taking that he would hereafter use for the entire expedition.

" While on the road, " he wrote later, " I always kept a little note pad five centimeters square, hidden in the palm of my left hand, and a two-centimeter stub of pencil in the other. I took down whatever struck me as I looked to the left or right. Whenever there was a change of direction I noted down the compass reading, also the contours of the land by means of barometric readings, the hour and minute of each observation, each stop made, the rate of speed, etc. I kept this up for the entire trip, and no one ever caught me at it, not even when I was with a large caravan. In such cases I had enough sense to walk either at the head or at the rear of the company. There with the help of my long, flowing garments, I was able to conceal the very slight movements of my hands. "

Whenever Charles arrived in the evening at some village and could get a room of his own, he recopied his notes into a permanent log of the journey, graphing a profile of the route taken during the day and making rough sketches of the topographical features.

An achievement more difficult than graphing the terrain and describing the route taken was the making of astronomical observations. The sextant was not as easy to hide as a compass, and it took a while to use it. What could he do?

" I could almost always take the elevation of the sun and the stars while staying in the villages, " he says. " During the day I would watch for that moment when no one was on the housetop of the place where I was staying. I would then carry the instruments up inside a bundle of clothing that I said I was going to spread out to dry. Mardochee would stand guard at the foot of the stairway, ready to engage in endless discussion anyone who might come and discover me. I would begin my observations whenever the surrounding housetops were also uninhabited, but even then I was apt to be interrupted. It was a long-drawn-out affair. "

More than once he was actually caught in the act, and to throw his discoverer off the track of his true purpose he would pose as a slightly demented astrologer. One time, for example, he said he was searching the heavens in order to discover the sins of the Jews; another time he confided to someone that with this equipment he could cast a spell to protect him from the cholera.

Finally on July 11th, beyond the endlessness of green plains, our travelers saw the battlements and red earthen walls of a city that was breathtakingly beautiful, with its lofty, white roof gardens, its gleaming green majolica shingles, its slender minarets rich with mosaics. Here was Fez in all its splendor, the religious capital of Morocco, and one of Sultan Moulay el Hasan's four brilliant political capitals.

But when they actually got to the city and inquired for the Jewish *mellah,* they found one of the most horrible and repulsive sights they had ever gazed upon. The ghetto was distinctly marked off from the city proper by a wide corridor of " no man's land " piled high with filth and putrefying animal carcasses that created an intolerable stench. This was the dump heap of Fez, located here to serve, unmistakably, as a racial boundary.

This ghetto had the narrowest, dirtiest, darkest

streets that Charles ever remembered seeing. He stumbled through them for quite a while before finding the evil-smelling basement entrance to the home of Samuel ben Simhoun, for whom he had a letter of introduction from the French legation.

But when the door was opened and Charles had groped his way through a hallway as dark as night itself, he was literally struck dumb by the enchanting panorama spread before him. He had entered a fabulous inner courtyard that seemed like a page out of the Arabian Nights. The inside walls rose for two stories, complete with exquisitely wrought balconies, and covered with mosaic from ceiling to ground level. The green-tiled fountain in the center of the court was a masterpiece of arabesque art. The owner of all this was a charming person and unusually well educated. He put " Rabbi Couvaud " in a cool little apartment, itself a work of ceramic art, and allowed him access to the roof garden, where the explorer could make his observations in full privacy.

But Foucauld had no intention of settling down in Fez. He made it plain that as soon as possible he must reach the Tadla, a vast, unexplored wilderness encircling the Middle Atlas Range. Ben Simhoun had just learned that Sheriff Sidi Omar was organizing a caravan bound for Bou-el-Djad, capital of the Tadla, and through his own private agency succeeded in getting a place in the caravan for his two guests.

By the time Charles left for Meknès, where he was due to join the caravan, his hair had grown down to his shoulders, putting him " in style " with Moroccan Jews. He then decided to shed the colorful Syro-Algerian garb he had been wearing, in favor of the more drab costume of a Moroccan rabbi (black headgear and black slippers) to reduce his visibility in the crowds.

On August 27th, at Meknès, Sheriff Sidi Omar broke trail with the long caravan, which included, besides our two rabbis, seven or eight wretched Moslems headed for the Tadla, two Jews of Bou-el-Djad returning home, and about fifty merchants whose destination was a bazaar being held about a day's journey away. They had plenty of excitement: in two hours' time they ran into five roadblocks set up by bandits, each band of marauders exacting a heavy " customs " fee.

Next day, after leaving the merchants to sell their oranges, olives, dates, and red peppers, and adding some reinforcements to their armed escort, the caravan started through a region of steep canyons carved out of the mountains. It was a densely wooded area, infested with hostile tribes. Fortunately these tribes did not stage any demonstrations, but the men accompanying them as escorts managed to drum up an incident of their own by throwing themselves on the ground and refusing to get up again until a substantial " bonus " was added to their pay. The bonus was forthcoming, and the caravan pressed onward through a multitude of frightening experiences, always tormented with the dread of an ambush. And every day the virus of fear kept eating away at poor Mardochee's strength.

On September 5th the caravan reached the Tadla. " We are only three hours' march from Bou-el-Djad, " Charles wrote in his notebook, " yet we have by no means arrived there yet. There are as many dangers in that little stretch of road as in all the way I have come so far. There is no more *anaïa* here, no more *zettet* that means anything. Everything is subject to raids, so that even a caravan armed with fifty rifles would hardly dare to venture out. "

There was only one expedient left — to appeal to Sidi ben Daoud, the only person who commanded any respect at Bou-el-Djad or in the entire Tadla. Charles remembered that at Tangier he had received from Moulay Abd es Selam, descendant of Mohammed and a friend of France, a letter of recommendation for this same Sidi ben Daoud, a descendant of that Omar who had been Mohammed's companion and the second caliph of Islam. At once he took one of his escorts, stripped the clothes form his back (his only safeguard against the greed of the bandits) and sent him into the fray armed with the letter — in search of Ben Daoud.

The following morning his messenger returned, fully dressed, accompanied by a handsome young man riding a white mule and shaded from the sun by a slave with an umbrella. This was Sidi Edriss, whose grandfather, Ben Daoud, had sent as an escort for the travelers.

When Charles and Mardochee reached Bou-el-Djad, they were taken to Sidi ben Daoud, a fine old man with a very light complexion, a kindly, honest face, and a long, white beard. They announced themselves as two rabbis from Jerusalem who had spent seven years in Algeria, etc., etc. Charles noticed that the old man eyed him very sharply, suspiciously. Mardochee noticed it too, and became so frightened that he lost his power of speech. But nothing happened to them. The grand old man gave orders that the two rabbis were to be put up in the finest style in the wealthiest Jewish home in the city.

In the days that followed, the two guests saw that they were being treated with every kindness, and they were invited with considerable regularity to lunch and dinner by the son and grandson of Ben Daoud. Such courtesies toward Jewish people were without precedent. What could it mean?

" It didn't take long for me to understand what was going on, " Foucauld wrote at the time, " because of two things I noticed. One of these was the frequency and amiability with which the members of Sidi ben Daoud's family entertained me. They sought to gain my confidence and get me to talk. The other observable phenomenon was the outright espionage engaged in by the Jews, who watched my every movement, insisted on reading my notes, and were always pawing over my instruments. Some little inkling must have come to Sidi ben Daoud, his son Sidi Omar, and his grandson Sidi Edriss, that I might be a Christian.

To test out their ideas, the *marabouts* have had the Jews keep an eye on us and have invited us out in order to keep us constantly under surveillance. "

Then the day came, during lunch, when Charles felt that young Sidi Edriss was about to lay his cards on the table — and he decided to play his own.

" You can't imagine how much I should like to visit France, " Sidi Edriss said nonchalantly.

" Nothing could be easier, " Charles assured him. " The French minister at Tangier could arrange for you to go to Algiers, and once you get there, I should be glad to put myself completely at your service. But would you be interested in bringing a Christian back to Bou-el-Djad? "

" Nothing would suit me better, provided he came disguised as a Moslem or a Jew, because the Sultan must know nothing about it, and my arrangements with the French Minister would have to be in the strictest confidence. "

" In that case, " Foucauld told him, " I am sure the French authorities would look with much more favor on the project, knowing that they could send French people to visit this city, because no Christian has ever been here. "

" That's not quite correct, " replied Sidi Edriss, with an enigmatic smile, " because Christians have already visited this city. "

" Disguised as Moslems? "

" No, as Jews. They did not give us their names, but we recognized them nonetheless. "

So then, Sidi Edriss, his father Sidi Omar, and his grandfather Sidi ben Daoud, already knew that he was a Christian! Would he be executed? No, for this devout family of Bou-el-Djad was an enemy of the Sultan's absolutist and isolationist despotism, and was seeking in as prudent a way as possible to establish contact with the Western world. And so Charles de Foucauld, masquerading as a rabbi, was given a letter conveying overtures of friendship, which he was to deliver to the French legation at Tangier.

Further steps in this romantic Moroccan expedition of the French Viscount and his Jewish guide brought them through the Grand Atlas Mountains, where nomadic tribes lived in tents, and through the Little Atlas, where the inhabitants clung closely to red-walled, battlemented *kasbahs,* constructed by their feudal lords at the summits of rocky crags, like eagles' aeries. Further south, the scrubby thickets of blackberry and acacia announced the nearness of the Sahara. They then ventured across the dunes of the Sahara itself, from the oasis of Tisint to that of Aqqa. Then, at last, they set their faces for home, proceeding from one forbidden city to another, from one hinterland to another, their itinerary bringing them at last to Mrimima, where some things happened that are worth mentioning.

The Christmas season had just passed — a gloomy Christmas for Charles de Foucauld, who experienced many nostalgic memories of childhood Christmases at Nancy, in the home of Grandpapà Morlet, retired artillery colonel. It was the day after Christmas, 1883 when Bou Rhim, an important citizen of Tisint and a close friend of Charles — his escort as far as Mrimima — placed the " two rabbis " under the protection of Sidi abd Allah, who was to escort them on the last leg of their journey. Sidi abd Allah was the superior of an important Moslem religious society at Mrimima, to all appearances an austere old patriarch, his bronzed face graced with a long white beard.

" I have never entertained any great sympathy with the Jews, " was the old man's opening remark to the two rabbis. " Nevertheless, since I have brought the two of you here as my guests, I will treat you with every respect. But in view of my feelings toward you Jews, the least I could ask you — as an act of kindness to repay me for the abhorrence I feel toward helping you — would be that you give me a little present, one suited to my dignity, quite apart from the tax already paid by you for the protection I am giving you. "

Charles felt he had gotten off easily when Sidi abd Allah was satisfied with two sugar loaves, some tea, and some cotton, which he collected from those who had been his escorts on the last trip. The holy man then excused himself, saying, " Very well, then. Now I will go to see someone who can furnish you with the escort. "

But how could this be? Wasn't the contract already " signed, sealed, and delivered? " Wasn't old Sidi abd Allah himself supposed to escort them on the next leg of their journey? Ah, the mysteries of forbidden Morocco!

The following day, which had been set for their departure, no one showed his face. Charles, who had found the atmosphere of Mrimima rather suspicious to begin with, decided to resort to " Plan B, " which was the best expedient — next to money — that one could resort to in this weird country. He rummaged through the various letters of recommendation supplied him before and during the expedition, and came up with one written by Moulay abd Selam, the highly respected sheriff of Ouezzan. It seemed the most likely to get him results.

The letter did create quite a stir, in fact. Scarcely had the host seen it, than he had it read publicly in the mosque, and for three days in a row Sidi abd Allah went out of his way to visit the two rabbis in person, and besides all this, he had two of his sons sleep with them every night, a very special guarantee to Charles and Mardochee of their safety and of the esteem in which they were held. But still, when the conversation got around to the matter of departure, the old man continued to be very vague. At last he secluded himself from them, pleading the excuse that he was not feeling well.

Meanwhile Charles had heard some very alarming news. Word was spreading through the whole territory that " Rabbi Couvaud " was really a disguised Christian, and was carrying a lot of money with him. At the Mrimima gates two rival bands of thieves (one of Arabs, the other of Berbers) stood ready to relieve him of his baggage whenever he set foot outside. Sidi abd Allah's embarrassment now had some explanations, and his pleas for patience seemed more justified.

New Year's Day, 1884, was as unhappy a time for Charles de Foucauld as Christmas had been gloomy. A few days later he heard that the Arab bandits had tired of their vigil and had gone away. The Berbers left too, but in their place came a band of about thirty men, the Aïn Seddrat gang. These cutthroats were less patient about waiting for their prey to come to them, and sent a delegation to Sidi abd Allah, hoping to intimidate the old man into giving them the custody of his guests.

For all his selfishness and other disagreeable characteristics, Sidi abd Allah now revealed himself as someone not totally dishonest. He gave the outlaws a blunt refusal and placed a guard around the two rabbis' dwelling to give them added protection.

The bandits sent a new embassy. The old dervish gave them just as negative an answer. The siege continued.

" There is only one solution, " Sidi abd Allah told his guests just after emerging from his diplomatic illness, " and that is to hold on another eight days, for at that time my entire religious confraternity will leave Mrimima with me on a holy pilgrimage to Tisint, where the great *marabout* is buried. During the great procession you could mingle with the crowds of pilgrims . . . . "

" Wait just a minute, " Charles broke in. " If you can't guarantee me the protection we agreed upon, so that I can leave here at once, then I must provide myself with other means for continuing the trip. "

And he sent a message to Tisint, to his friend Hadj Bou Rhim. Scarcely three days had passed when about 30 horsemen arrived, led in person by Hadj Bou Rhim. They entered Mrimima like a tempest, riding up at full speed to the place where Charles was staying.

Half an hour later the two rabbis were on their way to Tisint. The escort, that Hadj Bou Rhim had hastily recruited from among his relatives, was heavily armed, discouraging the Aïn Seddrat gang from any attempts to hold them up.

But the excitement was not yet over for Charles and Mardochee. Other misfortunes awaited them on the road from Tisint to El Outat, and even at Lalla Marnia on the Algerian border, where we find them on the morning of March 23, 1884 — unconscious, bruised, and bleeding.

Morocco had given them a very appropriate farewell, abusing and robbing them by the hands of the very men who had formed their last armed escort. As Charles wrote to his sister Marie, this was a land "where between the Sultan and the bandits neither rich nor poor have rest. Here authority defends no one, but threatens the possessions of everyone. Here the state continually collects taxes without ever spending anything for the good of the country. Here justice is bought and sold, crime is available for a fee, and the worker never receives his hire .... You work by day and stand guard at night. Close your eyes for an instant, and the thieves take your animals and yours crops .... And if by hard work and watchfulness you manage to reap your crops and get them into the granary, then you still have the Sultan to deal with. You want to claim exemption, so you complain of your misery, you say it was a bad year for farming. But the officials keep tabs on you. If they see that you do not buy grain when you go to the market (which shows that you have a good supply) then they will turn you in. Then one fine day a score of soldiers will swoop down upon you, search your house from top to bottom, confiscate your grain, everything. If you have slaves or animals, they will take them along too. In the morning you were wealthy, and by evening you are poor. But you must go on living. You must plant crops for next year, and there is only one place you can turn: to the Jew. If this particular Jew is an honest man, he will make you a loan at 60 per cent. If he is not, the rate will probably be much higher. And that is the beginning of the end, because the first year there is a drought, your property will be sold from under you and you will go to jail. After that, you are finished. "

On May 26, 1884, Charles de Foucauld reached Algiers and went at once to the library to see his old friend MacCarthy, turning over to him the notes he had compiled during the expedition. Then he put forever behind him the robe of the wandering Jew. But the Charles de Foucauld who emerged from that costume was still " the old man " to the nth degree. While the Algerian papers were publishing his discoveries, heralding them as a great triumph, he was submerging himself for twelve days in the most unrestrained orgies he had ever indulged in. But this was " the last fling " for the scion of the Viscounts of Foucauld de Pontbriand. The hour of his great transformation was at hand.

Mardochee received the payment agreed upon — 270 francs for each of the nine months the expedition had lasted — and in a short time he had blown it all on the pursuit of his life's passion: alchemy. Only a few months later, while conducting an experiment that he was sure would lead him to the philosopher's stone, he passed away, the victim of mercury-vapor poisoning.

The Road to La Trappe

The winter of 1888 was a hard one, even in Jerusalem. The housetops, the domes of the churches, the peaks of the minarets, the fronds of the palms and the branches of the olive trees, were all draped in white. The snowflakes were large, like the wings of butterflies, and the grimy streets of the old city became rivers of mud, now gray, now dark brown.

It was still snowing on Christmas Eve when a young European, sporting a handlebar mustache of the latest style and wearing an overcoat obviously of a Parisian cut, was seen braving the cold mud along the entire Via Crucis, all the way to Calvary. He then went to the Holy Sepulchre and walked through the Garden of the Resurrection. In the evening he came to Bethany, assisted at Mass, and received Communion. In the days following Christmas he visited Bethany and Cana, climbed Mt. Tabor, passed through Emmaus, and stopped at Nazareth. He spent extra time in Nazareth, walking the mud-filled streets crowded with children in rags.

He had already left Nazareth, when by impulse he returned, as though he heard a voice that refused to be ignored, saying, " Here, right here at Nazareth, is where Jesus lived for thirty years. He lived here in silence, unknown to the outside world, anonymous, praying with his mother and working at his father's carpenter shop. Thirty years. Does that mean anything to you? That is the length of life you have lived till now. It is also, perhaps, the length of life that remains to you. "

The way was now clear. Jesus had not called him to imitate His public life, and so had not directed him to some religious order wherein he might give himself to preaching or to intellectual pursuits. Nazareth spoke clearly to his heart. " Be hidden away in Jesus Christ, along with St. Paul, who ' chose to be despised ' because his Lord had been rejected of men. "

So this was the light — the light Charles de Foucauld had been seeking for four years, beginning, as we shall see, in the summer of 1885, when he lived at Tuquet, among the pleasant vineyards of Gironde.

Shortly after his journey through forbidden Morocco, which ended around the last of March 1884, Charles went to France. The reverberations from his accomplishments and the fame that had come to him, once the first official releases of his discoveries were made, had enabled his relatives to forget every trace of resentment they felt for the irregularities of his younger days. They received him with a heartiness that showed both pride and affection. Yet he found precious little time to spend with them.

By October he was back in Algeria to write up the notes on his Moroccan trip. The resulting book, published by Challamel with the title *Reconnaissance au Maroc*, was valuable as a scientific treatise, not to mention its literary excellence. The work was absorbing and demanding, but it still did not prevent him from involvement in a relationship that almost led to marriage, a marriage that would have had social complications from the very start. Fortunately his relatives intervened, indirectly, just in time to save him from this indiscretion. The key person in this act of redemption was his cousin Marie de Bondy, concerning whom we need to say a few words.

Aunt Inés, her beauty somewhat withered by this time, was by now the contented wife of good-hearted M. Moitessier. This was the same Aunt Inés who had been concerned about Charles' light-headedness, and even more about the way he spent his money, leading to the appointment of a legal guardian for him. She had two daughters. Catherine, the older of these, had married a professional diplomat, the Count de Flavigny. Marie, her second daughter, who had married Viscount de Bondy, was eight years older than Charles, and always had a soft place in her heart for her weird cousin, from the very moment his parents had died and left him an orphan.

Even during the many years when the Moitessier household was constantly snowed under with reports of the young man's misconduct, she alone, amid the consternation and indignation of the rest of the tribe, refused to say one word against him. In fact, she kept up a continual correspondence with Charles. Her letters, full of serenity and affection, had on a few occasions restrained him from some of the flagrant excesses he might otherwise have committed.

And even now her intervention, gentle and discreet, had dissuaded her cousin from his latest madness. " This was a marriage I needed to be saved from, and it was you who saved me, " he wrote. And this, as we shall see, was not to be the last time Marie de Bondy interfered in her cousin's life.

Meanwhile, in Algiers, Charles had fallen ill with a serious inflammatory disease. He called in a doctor, who firmly prescribed for his cure a long rest period in France, preferably in the country. It was the summer of 1885 when Charles, still feverish, arrived at the Moitessier estate at Tuquet in the Gironde, for a visit with his sister, who was living with her aunt there. " No work, no writing, no exertion whatsoever, " had been the Algerian doctor's orders, and Charles had no choice but to find a comfortable room and stay there — to think, and to watch what was going on. But, as his memoirs reveal to us, his every thought and his every feeling was directed toward the events of Africa.

The vineyards of Gironde are a refreshing sight, and to live there you need hire no one for " protection " nor pay for armed escorts, nor be on the lookout for ambushes, so important a part of life in Morocco.

But when the wind rustled the leaves of the grapevines, Charles heard instead the breezes swaying the palms of Tisint. And when through the window he saw the white beard of an elderly vineyard laborer, his thoughts turned to that noble patriarch, Sidi ben Daoud. And when at evening the sound of singing floated in from the distance, it seemed like the echo of Moslem prayers, broadcast from the remote ranges of the Atlas all the way to Gironde. He could see the worshipers, solemn, prostrate on the ground, calling out five times a day, *Allah' u akbar,* " God is greater! "

But at Tuquet he was soon to learn that not just the followers of Mohammed had faith or prayed, or worshiped in adoration. He was to learn that while the Bedouin bowed by the wayside on some faraway desert, his cousin Marie gave herself to prayer with at least as much abandon in the little village church nearby.

For years he had thought — from the time he had abandoned his faith almost 15 years earlier — that the differences between one religion and another were the best argument against religion as such. But now that he was acquainted with believers in both camps, he felt that his earlier conviction no longer held water, and that another attitude recommended itself to him — that from the burning Saharan sands and from the cool shadows of the Tuquet chapel there was really one act of faith that arose to God, one single hymn of praise that extolled the Most High.

Though he himself did not believe in this God, yet, without understanding it, he had an insistent urge to believe, for at a certain moment, his endless hours of enforced rest began to be filled with meditations on the world of faith and on the world of virtue. Of faith, he had none, it is true, but he could at least strive after virtue, even though it might be — at this stage — a pagan virtue.

So he set himself to seek for virtue, and he sought it first among the classical Greek and Roman writers. But they left him with a feeling of boredom and disgust. Then, almost by accident, he began looking at the work of a Christian author. It was Bossuet's *Elévation sur les Mystéres* which gave him his first appetite for the mystical approach to life, even though he was still shrinking away from actual faith in God, especially the Son of God. And the very thought of accepting " the yoke of the church " filled him with rebellion.

Meanwhile his health improved, and when the Moitessiers and his sister left for Paris in September, he returned to Algeria, with another expedition on his mind — a trip through the areas of Algeria most recently brought under the control of France. This he actually went through with, traveling from Mzab to El Goléa and working north to Tunisia, from which he sailed again for his homeland in January, 1886.

In Paris he established himself at No 50 Rue de Miromesnil, displaying in his new apartment all his preoccupation with Africa. Among the old family pictures on the wall was dispersed a complete gallery of exhibits depicting his "Moroccan sojourn." He acquired a collection of rare book editions, even hired a butler, but would not buy himself a bed, preferring to curl up on the rug, wrapped in his *burnous* — patterning after the sleeping habits of Hadj Bou Rhim and his friends "down under." Was this pure Bohemianism carried to exotic extremes? Or was it a kind of snobbish asceticism? Perhaps. Yet a comparison between the outlandish furnishings of a *pied-à-terre* in his earlier days and those of his present museum-home would be enough to show what sort of changes had already happened to Charles de Foucauld.

The Moitessiers lived on the Rue d'Anjou, only a short walk from Rue de Miromesnil. Aunt Inés' salon gatherings exerted a considerable influence on French politics of the day, and Charles was welcomed to this circle of notables with all the interest people normally have for one who has explored an unknown corner of the world. Yet he soon felt himself worked upon by a group of smooth operators trying to lure him into more " profitable " enterprises. But he felt only annoyance with the mirages they dangled before him and did not hesitate to show his lack of interest. The only reason he continued to hang around the salon was to be as often as possible with his cousin Marie, to whom he referred as " an angel on earth " and " the soul of piety. " Such epithets probably seem affected and amusing to the twentieth-century reader, as overworked as they are by poets and songwriters. But for Charles de Foucauld to utter them was something significant. A man such as he, who had for years " wasted his substance in riotous living, " measuring his relationships with women only in terms of his appetites and passions, could probably find no more accurate expressions for describing Marie de Bondy. For the first time in his life a woman who really incarnated virtue of the highest kind had come into his life, awakening in him a desire for moral purity that he had never felt before.

Another visitor to Aunt Inés and his cousin Marie in their home on the Rue d'Anjou was the Abbé Huvelin, himself a convert, and now vicar of St. Augustine's parish. Sickness and weight of responsibilities had left their telltale marks on his face, making him appear older than he really was. Many a man of the world came to hear him preach, though he was by no means one who offered the Gospel to the accompaniment of cherry brandy!

Charles warmed up to the Abbé at once, but without the faintest idea that this man could be of any help to *him*, of all people! If Cousin Marie had not yet succeeded in leading him back to the faith, Huvelin would certainly fare no better. This man was a priest, not a medicine man. And faith was not something that others could be hired to get for you, nor something you could buy on the open market. You couldn't even acquire it just to please someone as nice as Marie de Bondy.

" The decisive step, " writes the biographer Carrouges, " must be made in the secret recesses of the soul, as it steps over the threshold of a dark world of mystery. Everything is ready for Foucauld to take that plunge, but he doesn't. Yet every day he edges a little closer. Not only is he rereading Bossuet and understanding him better, but he is driven more to solitude and recollection. "

Then one day he entered the church of St. Augustine and walked slowly up and down in its subtle shadows, his lips quietly repeating. " My God, if you exist, let me come to know you. " Perhaps, with Pascal, we might inquire: Could he have sought for God, if he had not already found him?

But it is not easy for a man to comprehend what it is that moves him. Without denying anything to the sovereignty of grace, we know that for one who has lost his faith, it is not likely that he will recover it in one lightning stroke. Usually he must walk a long, painful road, where there are many steps forward and an occasional one backward, before he crosses the inner frontier and says his final yes of full belief.

In September, 1886, Charles de Foucauld went abroad again, to make a rapid Tunisian expedition, so that he could say he had explored all of North Africa from Tangier to Tunis. In October, just a month later, he could announce to Cousin Marie on his return to Paris that his mission was accomplished. But their conversation drifted inevitably to other subjects and closed with Charles' bitter comment: " You are a happy believer, but when I search for the light, I do not find it. "

But it was still only late October when, early one morning after a sleepless night, Charles de Foucauld left his home and went to the Church of St. Augustine. He didn't know, really, what he was looking for there; he only knew he needed help. He inquired for Abbé Huvelin in the sacristy; someone told him he was hearing confessions and pointed out which confessional box it was. Charles approached and spoke quietly from outside the confessional window; " Abbé Huvelin, I would like you to instruct me in the faith. "

" Kneel down, " said the quiet voice of the priest from out of the dark. " Confess to God and believe. "

" But that is not why I came. "

 " Confess, " the Abbé insisted.

A final moment of hesitation, then Charles entered the other side of the confessional and knelt with his face against the grating.

" Have you fasted? " the Abbé asked him shortly afterward. Charles answered him in the affirmative, and followed him to the Communion rail.

From then on he went almost daily to Communion, and every week he made his confession. His soul also began to experience a tranquillity it never knew before.

But Charles' conversion was not quite complete, because conversion means renewal of one's entire being, and he knew that this involved nothing less than total and absolute surrender of his whole life to God. " Once I believed that there was a God, " he wrote later, " then I knew there was nothing else to do but live only for Him. My religious vocation was born at the same instant as my faith. "

But in the meanwhile his fledgling faith was to find many obstacles against which it must battle for survival. For this neophyte in the faith the Gospel narratives still seemed, at times, rather fantastic. At other times he found passages from the Koran intruding into his prayers. His raw faith had to mature, and this required constant guidance from his confessor, and, which was even more important, the constant grace of God.

Yet in the midst of all his earlier confusion of thoughts, one idea constantly progressed and grew ever stronger from the moment Abbé Huvelin had pronounced his first absolution: " I want to be a religious, to live only for God, to do the perfect thing at any cost. "

But the Abbé made him postpone any decision until three years had passed. Meanwhile his desire to " vanish before God into pure nothingness " (suggested by the writer Bossuet) did not seem to find a very clear direction in his mind, and he had no idea what religious community he might choose.

It was a passage of the Gospel that gave him his first directive. What especially caught his attention was this: " You shall love the Lord your God with all your heart, and all your soul, and all your mind. This is the first and greatest commandment. And the second is similar to it: Love your neighbor as yourself. " Everything began with love and ended with it.

He found the second directive in a sermon preached in St. Augustine's by Huvelin, whose words he never forgot. " Our Lord chose the last place, and it was so low down that no one could ever take it from Him. " Charles agreed that *that* place could not be taken, but what would hinder him from taking the last place *left?* This was surely the best way to be close to Our Lord . . . .

For the next few months Charles de Foucauld, convinced that he now held the key to his own future, immersed himself in meditation on the

Great Paradox of Christianity: How can God be the Most High, while the Son of God has become " least " among men? A little at a time, he thought this through to clarity. The Most High had such a lofty love for humanity that it drove Him to conceal every telltale trace of His glory when He became man — the most sorrow-stricken of all men, even unto death on the cross — that He might earn the love of all men.

During these months no one could have realized what a spiritual spectacle was unfolding in this man's soul. He was still the elegant Parisian and a little on the snobbish side. He still frequented the salon of the Moitessiers, still kept a butler in the latest livery, and still inhabited rather weird quarters, where he spent most of his time correcting the proofs of his Morocco book and putting the finishing touches on his diagrams and maps. When the Challamel edition of *Reconnaissance au Maroc* finally came out, early in 1888, it met with almost fairy-tàle success, and the press prophesied " a brilliant future " for the author. Charles de Foucauld had to indulge in an ironical smile when he read about it.

Time passed, and in the summer of 1888 he was guest for several days at Chateau de Bondy on the Indre. It was while visiting there that he was counseled by Cousin Marie to visit the nearby Trappist monastery at Fontgombault. There he observed how the monks, clad in long garments of white wool, went about their work in silence.

He heard the blows of the hammer in the shop, the warbling of birds in the trees, the splashing of water in the fountain, the mooing of cows in the distance, the muffled drone of a bee in the garden, the sharp sound of a rake preparing the plowed earth — but in all this mysteriously serene little world, the human voice was never heard. And this pall of absolute silence, as it hung over human society, transfigured the French countryside, conferring on it the majestic muteness of the desert.

But even more impressive to Charles was the severely plain tunic, dirty and heavily patched, that he saw a brother wearing when he came in from work in the fields. For him it was the third directive to his thinking: *Here in this enclosure, as nowhere else* — thought he — *this brother has found " the lowest place, " and no costume in the world could be so becoming to him . . . .*

Was being a Trappist, then, the only way to fulfill his vocation? Back in Paris, he posed this question to his spiritual advisor. But Abbé Huvelin was not stampeded by Charles' enthusiasm. " Before making any decision, " he said, " it would be best to make a pilgrimage to the Holy Land, and there ask God to help you decide. "

We have already narrated, at the beginning of this chapter, what happened on that wintry trip to the Holy Land. After that decisive Christmas, Charles dreamed of nothing else than to live a life of silence, prayer, and work, as Jesus had lived for thirty years at Nazareth. This fourth directive was all he needed.

January 16, 1890, an especially windy day, found Charles following a wilderness path in the Vivarais highlands that led among beeches and firs, descending steeply to the Trappist monastery called Our Lady of the Snows.

There were two essential criteria by which he had appraised this particular community. First of all, it was the poorest of all the Trappist monasteries — and he desired to be the poorest among its poor monks. Secondly, this group of Trappists had founded a new monastery in Syria, near Alexandretta — and he hoped to be chosen as one of those sent to strengthen the new community, which would obviously be even poorer than the mother house.

Abbé Huvelin had heard his arguments, and — convinced that Foucauld was making a fully considered choice — gave his approval. It was the moment of final decision.

Several months intervened between the moment of his final choice and his actual admission to " La Trappe " (a name sometimes used for the Order, after the place in Normandy where the first Trappist community began). During these months of waiting, the court at Nancy made a decision that returned to Charles the legal custody of his own finances. What a strange history this Foucauld fortune underwent! At a time when it was unwise for him to have it, he was given full possession. When he was ready to make responsible use of it, only a small pittance was doled out to him by a guardian. Now the complete control of it had been returned to him, just at the moment when he had lost all interest in keeping it. And so now he gave his entire estate to his sister.

After a final tour of farewell visits to his relatives, from Nancy to Dijon and on to Paris, he spent the eve of his parting with cousin Marie de Bondy. They assisted at a Mass celebrated by Abbé Huvelin and received Communion together. Finally, after one last embrace of his kinfolk on the Rue d'Anjou, he left on foot, alone, for the railway station.

The forest was behind him, but the wind murmured as much as ever along the treeless descent of the mountain, as Charles lifted up his eyes and beheld the white granite wall of the lonely monastery. He felt in that moment that everything was finished: the silliness of Saumur, the amours of Evian, the fabled fortunes of Fez, the comradeship of Bou-el-Djad and Tisint, the gentle passions of Paris; Moroccan nights under a sky of crystal clearness; Parisian nights illumined by the lamps of the great boulevards; summers among the vineyards of Gironde and at the Indre chateau.

At the same time he felt that everything was just *beginning* here now, in this domain of silence.

He rang the bell at the gate. " I should like to speak with Father Abbot, " he said, and the brother doorkeeper wordlessly conducted him to Dom Martin.

"What can you do?" he was asked almost at once.

"Very little."

"Then take this." And the Abbot gave him a broom.

"It is better to take the last place when and where God wills it," was Charles' soft response.

On the 27th of that same month he began community life as a postulant. Ten days later he took the habit worn by "novices of the choir" — a full-length tunic of white wool, a hood, and a cloak. The Viscount de Foucauld de Pontbriand chose as his religious name Brother Marie-Alberic. "Marie," he explained, was for the Virgin of Nazareth; for his cousin, who had been such an inspiration to him; and for his sister, toward whom he had the tenderest affection. "Alberic" was the name of one of the holy founders of the Cistercian Order.

At Our Lady of the Snows, every day was the same as the last. For Brother Marie-Alberic a day meant prayers, study, sweeping the floors, and a hungry homesickness for his loved ones, Marie, Catherine, his sister, his aunt . . . .

"We rise at 2 A.M." he wrote to his sister. "We go to the church, where we recite the psalms out loud in choir for two hours. Then there is an hour to an hour and a half of free time. We read or pray; the priests celebrate their Masses. About 5:30 we begin reciting Prime in choir, then comes community Mass. After that we go to the chapter-house for some prayers. The Superior comments on a passage from the Rule, and if someone has committed an offense he confesses it publicly and receives a penance, which is never very severe. Then more free time — 3/4 of an hour — to read and pray, followed by the third " choir. " Then, about 7:00, our work begins, the specific task having been assigned by our Superior as we emerge from the third choir. The work continues until 11:00, when we go again to choir for Sext. At 11:30 we go to the refectory. After a meal, monastic style, we go to our rooms to sleep until 1:30 P.M. There is a three-quarter-hour interval after this, for individual prayers and reading. At 2:30 is Vespers. After Vespers we work till a quarter of six. At 6:00 there are prayers. At 6:15, dinner. Then there is a little free time till 7:15, when there is reading for the whole community in the chapter-house. Then there is Compline, the singing of the *Salve*, and bedtime. We go to sleep at 8:00. "

The Trappists have no separate cells, but sleep all together in a simple dormitory. For Charles it was farewell to the comforts of his family, farewell to Room 82 at Saumur with its sofas and deck chairs, farewell to the *garconnière* at Pont-à-Mousson, farewell to Paris apartments and Moroccan tents.

But why had he chosen La Trappe? " It was for love, only for love, " he wrote.

Perfection at Any Cost

The envelope was like a great pennant of brightly colored stamps, each bearing the Turkish crescent. Marie de Blic, *nee* Foucauld, had waited several months for the letter it contained. One passage especially impressed her: " For us the heaviest work is the kind we do out in the fields. In winter we trim the trees; in spring the vines must be pruned; summer is the time for cutting hay and harvesting grain. We finished harvesting just the other day. Ours is the work of a peasant, in other words, work that is infinitely good for the soul, providing opportunity for prayer and meditation. It is heavier work than could be imagined, especially for someone like me who has never done it before. It gives you such a compassion for the poor, such charity for the working man, such love for the laborer! One realizes the true price of a piece of bread, when it costs him so much sweat to produce it. You learn early to have pity on the man who works with his hands, after you have partaken of his kind of work. "

The letter was signed by Mme. de Blic's brother, once know as Viscount Charles de Foucauld de Pontbriand, but now simply as Brother Marie-Alberic. It had come from faraway Syria, from the Trappist monastery of Our Lady of the Sacred Heart, at that time within the borders of the Ottoman Empire. It was dated late in the summer of 1891. Charles, as the family continued to call him, had now been away for over a year.

Brother M. Alberic had actually spent only six months in the French Trappist community of Our Lady of the Snows among the frozen hills of the Vivarais. " He was like an angel in our midst, " the Abbot, Dom Martin, wrote of him. But since they did not want him to pine too long for the extremely poor community in Asia Minor he so much longed to join, in June 1890 he was allowed to lay down his novice's broom, travel to Marseilles, and catch a boat for the Near East. On July 9th, he landed at Alexandretta beneath a glowing sky and was met by Father Etienne, who wore a long white wool tunic splattered with mud. In silence they mounted a pair of mules, and were escorted on the first leg of their journey by a platoon of Turkish gendarmes. After that, accompanied by a patrol of Kurdish soldiers, they headed further inland.

The road climbed steeply through the Alma Dag Mountains, while high above them the ghostly towers of ancient castle ruins stood guard along the cliffs. The winding trail reminded him of some rugged patches of terrain in the Little Atlas. The armed escort proceeding cautiously beside them; the horsemen with their shifty eyes who kept crisscrossing their line of march; those caravans, moving with exasperating slowness, and forever bogging them down; the dense forests infested with bandits, making it impossible to set foot off the trail: all these things made Charles de Foucauld feel that he was reliving some episode of his Moroccan adventure. Only the clothes he wore — the Cistercian habit of Brother Marie-Alberic, instead of the picturesque costume of " Rabbi Couvaud " — kept him from feeling he had just woken up after a long sleep to find himself, some years back and thousands of kilometers away, on some forbidden trail in the land of Sultan Moulay el Hasan.

They rode for two days and nights, with brief stops for catnaps. Upward they crawled to the summit, of the Syrian Gates, and descended on the other side of the pass to the village of Akbès, which looks out over a breathtaking precipice. They plummeted down a steep mule trail, hardly marked in the rocks, into an abysmal gorge. After a long ride through this narrow gulley, they climbed out through a dry creek bed, emerging at last into a wide valley that spread out invitingly at an altitude of 2,500 feet, encircled by impenetrable mountains. Here were gray granite peaks honeycombed with caverns, their outer slopes covered with pinasters, giant oaks, and wild olive trees. Here was pasture for partridges and deer, a hideout of bandits, and in the wintertime a hunting ground for wolves, panthers, bears, and wild pigs.

If the scenery along the route from Alexandretta had reminded Charles of some inaccessible areas in Morocco, this valley that loomed up so unexpectedly — with its green pastures, its golden grain, its variegated orchards — transported him as on a magic carpet to his childhood home in the Vesges, when he used to walk hand in hand with good old grandpapà Morlet, retired artillery colonel.

But two visible phenomena helped bring the young novice back to rough reality. One of these was a high, massive stockade, latticed with blackberry bushes, enclosing the entire valley at the forest's edge. It was built to prevent the incursion of wild animals. The other item that arrested his attention was the village in the center of the clearing. Its wood and mud barracks and thatched roofs reminded Charles of photographs he had seen — pictures of settlements in the American West that housed the sourdoughs prospecting for gold.

So this was Our Lady of the Sacred Heart! " It is a great confusion of barns, cattle, houses built back to back — for fear of guerrillas and robbers — all in the shade of immense trees, " Charles wrote in a letter, adding: " Thirty years ago this was a well-inhabited place, whereas now it is a wilderness. In the process of putting down a rebellion, the

Turks razed the place to the ground; they did not realize they were getting it ready for *us.* ”

It was in 1882 that the Trappists of Our Lady of the Snows, facing possible expulsion from France, had sent some of their members here to establish an asylum. One of their number had discovered the appropriate refuge in Syrian territory, in this little hollow, hidden away in the mountains. Here the wrath of the Turks had cut a swath of destruction, leaving behind no trace of men or their possessions.

Then a few other monks had come from France to found this new offspring of La Trappe, dedicated to Our Lady of the Sacred Heart. Dom Louis Gonzaga, a brother of Dom Martin, became its prior. Some Kurds came down out of the mountains and were persuaded to give up their predatory way of life; then, all together, they went to work. They put up some emergency housing, they enclosed the valley with a wall, they tore down the ruins of the earlier settlement and cultivated it with spades and hoes. And with every passing year the ground had yielded a little more malt, a little more grain and wood, a little more grapes and cotton, an ever more abundant harvest.

Now after eight years of unrelenting work, there was something about the delightful little valley, with its tidy pastures and straight rows of grain, that enchanted the eyes of Charles de Foucauld. But the monastery — if this is proper

terminology for that jumble of miserable shacks —
still looked like the set for a Western movie. In
summer the Brothers slept in an area that doubled
for a hayloft, just above the community stables.
The odor of manure drifted up through the loose
floorboards, and the constant movements of the
animals gave them no peace all night. When winter
came they slept in a different hayloft, this one
above the refectory, where the freezing cold
penetrated the snow-covered, sheet-metal roof.

" There are about twenty Trappists here,
including the novices, " Charles wrote a short
time later to his sister, Marie de Blic. " We have
cattle, oxen, goats, horses, and donkeys. In other
words, we do our farming on a large scale. In the
barracks we house about a score of Catholic
orphans, ranging in age from 5 to 15; about 15 day
laborers (the Kurds who had been converted from
banditry to agriculture); also a continually fluctuat-
ing number of guests — in the real meaning of that
word — because, as you know, the monastery is a
place where hospitality is practiced . . . . My soul
experiences a profound peace, a peace that has
never forsaken me since I arrived, and that grows
with the passing of time, although I realize how
little it is of my own doing and how much it is a
pure gift from the Lord. "

Poverty sanctified by prayer, labor rendered
sacred by the Rule, in the land called Asia where
the first Christian hermits had lived — all this
moved him so profoundly that for a while he

actually believed that he had recovered all the simplicity of the primitive Church.

But then he remembered what still linked him to the present world — his rank as a reserve officer in the army and his extravagant apartment at 50 Rue de Miromesnil in Paris. Hastily he wrote his sister, pointing out that the apartment was also hers, as a gift. Following that, he wrote to the Minister of War, requesting a final discharge from the French Army. Then, with a sigh of relief, he wrote to Cousin Marie de Bondy: " The step I have now taken gives me true joy. I had already given up every possession, except for some little impediments that remained to heckle me: my officer's rank and a little piece of property. But now, glad to say, I am rid of them. "

On the morning of February 2, 1892, before dawn had yet announced the feast of Candlemas, Brother Marie-Alberic took the vows of poverty, chastity, and obedience in the Order of Reformed Cistercians, better know as the Trappists. " So now I no longer belong to myself at all, " he wrote that same evening. " I find myself in a state such as I was never in before, except on my return from Jerusalem. I feel the need for recollection, for silence, to rest at the feet of God and behold Him. "

" I would like you to know, dear lady, " wrote Dom Louis Gonzaga, the Trappist prior, to Marie de Bondy, " what a holy traveling companion has now joined us on our journey to heaven . . . . Our venerable Father Polycarp, who is his spiritual director, with fifty years of religious profession and thirty of spiritual supervision behind him, assures me that never before in his long life has he come across a soul so completely dedicated to God. "

He also confided in her, perhaps in order to enlist her help: " I would like Brother Marie-Alberic to study theology and become a priest, but I can see that I will have no easy job reconciling this with his humility. "

If that was the wish of Dom Louis Gonzaga, it was even more the contemplated goal of his brother, Dom Martin. The latter, having come from France on a canonical visit to the Syrian community, told his fellow prior quite frankly that Brother Marie-Alberic was the man most qualified to succeed him as spiritual head of his monastery, Our Lady of the Sacred Heart. But both of them agreed that it would not be easy to convince Brother M. Alberic of this.

As for the subject of all this maneuvering, he entertained no such " holy ambition. " Or perhaps we should say that the one legitimate, unwavering ambition that he did entertain was to seek, always and everywhere, the very last place. The two Superiors found immediate evidence of this when they began their first probings. At once he declared himself unworthy of the priesthood, and deliberately rejected the idea of any dignity, however purely religious it might be, being conferred on him. It was the same firmness with which he was henceforth

72

to resist any temptation to leave his " lowest place, " ✓
because, as he said, this was the only way he could
feel close to Christ. " I find my liveliest joy comes
from remaining completely abandoned to these
fields and forests, and I have nothing but contempt
for anything that could estrange me from this last
place I have chosen for myself, or from the attitude
of humility that I would like always to deepen
according to the example of Our Lord. "

The " danger " of becoming a priest (as
Brother Marie-Alberic described it) still seemed at
a safe distance, however, after the matter of theological studies was completely hushed up and he
was assigned the duty of mending and patching the
clothes of the community's orphan population.
Now he actually felt like he could reach up and
touch heaven, so close did this work seem to bring
him to the little cottage in Nazareth!

But his happiness was short-lived. In August,
1892, he was ordered to lay down needle and
thread and begin his study of theology. He appealed
desperately, persistently, to the Prior. " I have no
such vocation! " But Dom Louis Gonzaga replied
dryly that the decision had already been made.

For a few days Brother Marie-Alberic seemed
completely crushed by what had happened. But
then he remembered that perfect obedience has
more purity than the purest of personal intentions.
So twice a week, accompanied by another Trappist,
he made the long trip to Akbès, through the gaping
gorge and over the maddening mule trail that was
scarcely a dent in the perpendicular cliffs above

and below it. There, in the Lazarist mission, he received lessons from the superior, Father Destino, whose father had been one of the King of Naples' ministers, and who had himself already served as professor of theology at Montpellier.

" I find theology interesting, " he wrote a while later. But he never expressed a real love for it. He was interested in it insofar as it spoke of God, and brought him closer to Him. But as science, insofar as it is not part of life itself, not an act of love — it never aroused any excessive enthusiasm on his part. " These studies, " he wrote, are worth less than the practice of poverty, obedience, self-denial, and the imitation of Our Lord; whereas manual labor leads to the possession of these. Nevertheless, since this is something I am doing out of obedience, after having done all I could to resist it, this is evidently what the Lord requires of me at this moment. "

During the trips between the monastery and the Lazarist mission at Akbès, Charles de Foucauld had plenty of time to think over the events of his life. Little by little he began to feel less happy with himself.

He remembered having written to someone earlier: " The more I give to God, the more He gives in return. I thought when I lost the world that I had given everything away. But when I entered La Trappe, I received more than I had given. " He knew he had written these lines out of an overflow of joy. But now those very words were what unsettled him. He had dreamed of a community poorer and more rigorous than any other in the world, and now that he had found it, it in turn seemed too nice, too easy . . . .

The order to study began to be a problem to him also. " Alas, in order to apply myself fully to my studies, I am forced to give up all my reading and to spend less time in the church . . . . Theology is interesting, yes, and can even be a pleasant pursuit at times . . . , but how much did St. Joseph know about such things? " He found himself pondering the irony of his own predicament: a Trappist monastery that asked him to commit himself to the goal of academic attainments was more than he had bargained for. He would also constantly hear the haunting refrain of words spoken by St. Vincent de Paul: " Let us love God, yes, let us love God, but in the strength of our arms and the sweat of our brow. "

To add to Charles' already growing sense of discomfort, in April, 1893, Pope Leo XIII issued a Brief, authorizing Trappists to use oil and butter as condiments for their vegetarian diet. The " authorization, " in fact, had the force of a recommendation. He understood very well that the Pope's main concern in issuing the document was to protect, as much as possible, the health of Trappist monks. And he knew too that Our Lady of the Sacred Heart would make such a change only to conform to the policies dictated by Rome. Yet all this did nothing to decrease his misgivings that as a member of the Trappists he was becoming more and more like a fish out of water. And so the ex-connoisseur of gastronomic delicacies could write to Marie de Bondy: " For several weeks now we have not had the good old salt-and-water cooking . . . . The food has had an enormous amount of grease put into it lately . . . . You have no idea how unhappy it makes me. Less mortification means that we give a little less to God, and a little less to the poor. "

As time passed, his restlessness increased, until he felt he must boldly face up to the dramatic question now uppermost in his thoughts: Could he, should he, remain any longer with the Trappists? Until now, it was true, he had only made a temporary vow, but this was small consolation to him in his anguish.

He now decided to ask the advice of Father Polycarp and his Superiors, which he did with all frankness. " I am now convinced, " he told them, " that my vocation does not coincide completely with that of the Order of Reformed Cistercians. "

When he was asked to specify to what other Order his vocation seemed to be calling him, he said he did not think at the moment there existed in the Church any community quite like the one he wanted to belong to. " Seeing that it is not possible in a Trappist community to live the same life of poverty, of abnegation, of concrete detachment, of humility, and of recollection, that Our Lord did at Nazareth, I have had to ask myself whether He has given me all these lively desires so that I might merely offer them up as sacrifices, or if, in the absence of such a congregation in the Church today — one that offers the possibility of a life such as He lived in this world — I ought not to seek out other souls with whom I could found a little group of this kind. We would follow the life of Our Lord as exactly as possible. We would live only by the works of our hands, accepting neither gifts nor alms, following all the evangelical counsels to the letter, possessing nothing, giving to anyone who asks of us, not claiming anything for ourselves, depriving ourselves of everything we can in order to be as much like Our Lord as possible and to give as much as possible to Him in the person of the poor. To our work we would add many prayers, although we would not recite the Office in choir, because this would be an obstacle in the treatment of our guests and contributes little to the sanctification of those who are not learned. We would form, in other words, little groups, little 'dovecotes' or 'Carmels' — because large monasteries almost of necessity acquire material importance, and this becomes opposed to the ideals of abnegation and humility. And thus we could spread everywhere, particularly in pagan or especially forsaken territories, where one could all the more willingly help to increase the presence of love and the number of those who serve Our Lord Jesus. "

This he told his Superiors, but of his confessor he asked from whence came these desires of his to realize the " ideal of Nazareth? " Were they from God, from the devil, or from his own fantasies? " Father Polycarp told me not to think about it any more for the moment, but to wait for the right opportunity — which God would most certainly provide, if my desire were actually from Him. "

Abbé Huvelin's reply to his request for counsel was a little more animated than that of his confessor: " Keep up your theological studies, at least until you are made deacon; apply yourself to the exercise of interior virtue, and especially humility. As for the external virtues, practice those through perfect obedience to the Rule and to your Superiors . . . . As for anything further, we'll have to wait and see. Moreover, you know that it is not at all in your makeup to be a leader of others. " And Brother Marie-Alberic bowed assentingly to this reply.

" Patience, more patience," he would keep murmuring to himself, and that patience became all-important to him during the next several months when God gave him no sign whatsoever of His will. But the " signs " were on their way.

The first breakthrough was in April, 1894. Brother Marie-Alberic had been given orders to go to a nearby house and sit vigil with the corpse of an Arab Catholic worker. The minute he stepped inside the dead man's hut, he was struck to the quick. A few minutes' walk away from the poorest Trappist monastery in the world, he had discovered

poverty so overwhelming that it made the " poverty "
of the monks seem like sheer luxury.

We Trappists — he thought to himself — have
given up the world, it is true; no doubt we have a
tough life; but the man who lived and died here
has led a harder life than ours. Besides, we brothers
are part of a large community, so that we can help
each other out. We have a little land, and a little
livestock, but this man had to support his family
all alone, like St. Joseph. He had no possessions,
and he has survived this long only because every day
he earned what little he could by working with his
hands. " How different his house and mine . . . .
And how I long for Nazareth! "

A year later, in November 1895, there was a
great massacre, and this was Charles' second
" sign. " The Armenian Christians rose against the
Turks, and the Turks used this as an occasion to
make a great slaughter — not only of Armenians,
but of all the Christians, Catholic or Orthodox,
wherever they could find them. In a few months
the number of victims had mounted to 140,000
(at Marash, the city closest to the monastery, 4,500
were killed in two days) and many of these were
genuine martyrs, because they had died willingly,
without defending themselves, rather than deny
the faith.

" The Europeans are protected by the Turkish
government, so we are quite safe, " Charles
complained bitterly. " But it is a very disheartening
thing to be treated thus by the very people who
cut our brothers' throats. How much better to

perish along with them than to be protected by their assassins! "

This great tragedy further frustrated his desire for total abnegation. If he had not been committed to complete obedience, the stockade surrounding the little green valley could not have contained him for a minute.

But he still obeyed, still humbled himself by means of that obedience. Although for three years he had longed to leave the monastery, yet out of a desire for obedience he renewed his temporary vows for another two years, beginning January 1896. But at the same time he was working out, to the minutest detail, a proposed rule for the little communities he dreamed of founding and to which he had already given a name: Congregation of the Little Brothers of Jesus.

These communities, he said, are to be established in neighborhoods and suburbs of the larger population centers, or at least in those sections where the very poorest people live. They will live in small habitations that must be comparable to the very poorest homes in that area, perhaps just a shed or lean-to. Each dwelling is to contain three rooms, one of them to be used as a chapel, the second as a guest room, and the third for the Little Brothers. No chairs, no beds; just some rough benches along the walls. Nearby there could be a little garden to raise vegetables, perhaps even a little fruit. The rules of enclosure would be very strict, and silence must reign perpetually, to be broken only by prayer. Prayer and work are to be the two activities of each day; the work is to be manual and of the very simplest kind. This will permit identification with the very lowest class of people, and will also leave the spirit free for meditation. The worker's wage is to be the very lowest paid, and his costume is to be that of the very poorest people of that country. Two meals will be sufficient for nourishment, one of cereal, cooked with water and salt, the other a pound of bread. Only on Sundays can there be a little milk or honey, a pat of butter, and some fruit. But for those who are sick, nothing is to be spared. " Let them have an abundance of good things. " Even prayers come under the " poverty " category. The brother will assist at Mass, adore the Blessed Sacrament, recite the Angelus, the Stations of the Cross, and the Rosary, but not the Office. No one is to be excluded from prayers because he does not know Latin.

Charles de Foucauld gave Abbé Huvelin a copy of his proposed rule. The answer, expressing clearly the writer's alarm, came by return mail: " Your rule is absolutely impracticable. If the Pope had hesitations about approving the Rule of St. Francis because he thought *it* too rigorous, then you can imagine how *yours* would fare! Do you want me to be honest with you? It frightens me. Go live, by all means, at the outskirts of some community and practice all the humility you care to, but please, I beg of you, don't write any more rules. "

Poor Abbé Huvelin! What a blow he got from reading that rule! But he had done something useful nevertheless. He still refused to recognize in Charles de Foucauld the qualities necessary for the founder of an order, but he had finally conceded him the right to leave the Trappists and to live as a lonely " fool for God " at the edge of some monastery.

Charles picked up the ball and ran with it. First he presented his request to Father Polycarp, then to his Superiors, who contacted Rome, asking authorization from Dom Sebastian, the Superior General of the Trappists. But when the answer arrived, on September 10, 1896, all it said was that Brother Marie-Alberic should leave at once for the Trappist community of Staouëli, where he would receive further instructions.

Staouëli is located on a desert plateau, ten miles uphill from Algiers. Its Prior, at the moment, was that same Dom Louis Gonzaga who up till recently had been director of the Syrian monastery of Our Lady of the Sacred Heart.

Charles felt a great joy to see his beloved Africa after ten years, and to greet his old Superior. But it was a short-lived pleasure, dispelled as soon as he was given the " further instructions " from Dom Sebastian. His final test would be to study theology for two years in Rome. Two years! He was already 38 years old, and for over three years he had borne patiently one trial after another. But obedience came to his rescue yet once more. We even find him writing that " to obey is to love; in fact, it demonstrates the purest, the most perfect, the most sublime, the most disinterested, the most reverent kind of love. "

In November, 1896, Charles arrived at Rome and took up lodging at the general headquarters of the Reformed Cistercians, near St. John Lateran. Shortly afterward he began his studies at the Gregorian University.

" Now, " he wrote, " I must lay manual labor completely aside. We are still not mature enough to work like St. Joseph. We must first learn to read, as the Boy Jesus did. "

Meanwhile the most dreaded of dates approached, February, 1897 — the fifth anniversary of his taking the first Trappist vows. The Constitutions of the Trappists required that Charles must by then either take perpetual vows or else leave the Order. The date occurred during his last test of obedience, and it was this that complicated everything. If he left the Trappists, he would feel he " didn't have what it takes. " If he confirmed his vows, then he would close the door forever on any other possibilities that God might be calling him to.

It was Dom Sebastian who finally resolved the dilemma in the nick of time. He called an emergency session of the Council, and the two years of theology were wiped off the slate. Brother Marie-Alberic was free to go where he wished, with the sole request that he ask counsel from Abbé Huvelin before taking his next step. The Abbé would once again be his only spiritual director.

" I believe that the direction of my vocation is downward, " Charles wrote to him. " Now I am no longer obliged to be a conventual religious, and I can gravitate downward to the rank of handyman and servant. " That is to say, he wanted to occupy the lowest place, even in the ecclesiastical world.

The Abbé, in his reply, repeated his permission to let Charles live in all the obscurity he desired for himself, as long as he stayed at the gate of a convent. But again he enjoined him, in the strongest terms possible, not to write up rules for anyone else!

It was still September when Charles de Foucauld left Rome, furnished with a little pocket money by the Trappists — just enough, in fact, to put him on a boat for Jaffa. From Jaffa he would go to Nazareth, and there seek to live " the life of Nazareth. "

The Marabout of the Red Heart

On the morning of March 6, 1897, Sister Marie Fidele of the Poor Clares of Nazareth spent a longer time than usual at the convent chapel. She had pretended to leave with the other nuns after prayers were over, but instead she hid herself behind a pillar, where she could keep her eye on a strange tramp kneeling before the tabernacle.

He had come to the chapel at a very early hour (*probably up to no good,* she thought) dressed in rags and covered with dust. His beard was untrimmed, his feet swollen and bloody from walking in sandals with the bottoms worn through (*this fellow must have really been hiking!*), on his head he wore something in between a beret and a turban, and his other clothes consisted of a blue and white striped smock, hanging flappily over his cotton trousers, which were probably also some shade of blue. *This is the kind you have to watch,* thought Marie Fidele, *or he may take off with the gold monstrance.* So she stood guard while the sinister figure at the altar remained immobile, as though determined never to take his eyes off the tabernacle. When, three hours later, he finally stirred a little and stood up, the nun thought " Now he'll try something, " and got ready to sound the alarm. But the vagabond, unaware of being watched, left the chapel and went at once to the gate of the convent.

He rang the bell, and the porter, Sister Martha, was surprised to hear such a poorly dressed man ask her in perfect Parisian French, " I'd like to speak to the Mother Superior."

At this point in our story I suppose not even the display windows of Paris's largest second-hand store could have handled an exhibition of all the costumes and uniforms worn during his life by the Viscount Charles de Foucauld de Pontbriand. But such an exhibit, if arranged chronologically, would make a good commentary on the various phases of this man's life history. Let's see: At 8 years of age he wore the uniform of the Diocesan College of Strasbourg. At 18 it was the cadet uniform of St. Cyr Military School. Here he is at 20 years of age — in the costume worn by students of the Cavalry School in Saumur. At 21, he wears the Hussar sub-lieutenant's uniform. (Oh yes, and we would have to display his " night uniform " for his " other life " during this period — white tie and tails will do.) Then at 22 we have the colonial sub-lieutenant's uniform that was worn in the African Rifle Regiment. At 25 we have the Syro-Algerian get-up worn by " Rabbi Joseph Aleman of Moscow." And a short time later we have the more modest Morocco-Jewish costume of "Rabbi Couvaud." For age 32 we could use a Trappist's robe to remind us of Brother Marie-Alberic, as he was called during that period. After seven years of this, we find him leaving La Trappe and once more changing his name — to Brother Charles of Jesus. And for this new epoch in his life (now under discussion) there is a representative costume also — that of the poorest beggar of Palestine. Only one thing distinguished him from other beggars: a rosary with large beads that he wore around his waist.

He had left Jaffa on February 24th without a penny in his pocket, and had walked south, as a pilgrim to Bethlehem and then to Jerusalem. Heading north, he reached Nazareth, fulfilling a dream of long standing. In eight days he had walked about 125 miles.

The traveler who arrived at Nazareth was almost starved, physically exhausted, his clothes in tatters and leaving tell-tale stains of blood on the narrow streets. He presented himself to the Franciscans of Casa Nova, asking for a little work and permission to live at the gate of the monastery (in accordance with Huvelin's precise recommendation, that he live " at the edge of some religious community.") But the good friars had no work to offer him. He would have to appeal to the Poor Clares.

And now, here he was, in their whitewashed reception room, furnished with a table and a chair. Behind an iron grating hung a black curtain that left no opening. From behind that curtain a woman's voice spoke gently: " Jesus Christ be praised."

Brother Charles did not give any autobiographical information, but abruptly made a simple request for work. Mother Saint Michel said at once that she needed someone to act as sacristan, to run some errands, and to do some fairly menial odd jobs. How much would he expect to be paid for such work? On hearing his reply the Mother Superior suspected at once that this was no ordinary applicant for work: " I don't need any wages. Just give me a little bread and water and some free time when I can pray."

He refused to live in the regular gardener's quarters, preferring the wooden tool shed at the end of the garden, which was scarcely larger than a sentry's shelter. To put it in shape for residence he did some housecleaning, bricklaying, and carpentry. A Sister brought him a little table, a bench, and a straw mattress. But the mattress stood unused in a corner; he preferred sleeping on the ground.

The remodeling finished, he conferred upon his dwelling the exalted title of " hermitage " and dedicated it to Our Lady of Perpetual Help.

Thus began the new phase in Foucauld's life, and a new daily schedule: up before dawn, walk to the Franciscan friary, in prayer there until 6. Back to the convent to clean up chapel and prepare altar. Serve for chaplain's Mass at 7, put church in order afterward.

For the rest of the day he spaded the garden or watered plants, and whatever odd jobs one finds to do around a convent. He also went after the mail, because in those days there was a Nazareth post office but as yet no delivery service. His free moments he dedicated to prayer in the chapel or to reading in his living quarters. His reading diet consisted of devotional books, loaned to him by the nuns, and works of theology sent him by his relatives in France.

Sunday was the only time he would share the scanty menu of the Poor Clares; every other day, on weekdays, he limited himself to hard bread and water.

After the Mother Superior found out, through the other Sisters, what he was eating, she frequently gave orders for some almonds and dried figs to be sent him as appetizers. But she eventually found out that he always hid these goodies in a box and then gave them away to children and beggars when he thought no one was looking.

Mother Saint Michel finally discovered (through what source we do not know) the true identity of Brother Charles of Jesus. Out of respect for his vow of silence and his desire to be let alone, she did not breathe a word of it to anyone. But she decided to put him to the test.

The feast of the Transfiguration (August 6th) was approaching and every year it was the custom of most Christians living in and around Nazareth to make the two-hour climb up Mount Tabor as a pilgrimage. But as was customary, the pilgrimage would degenerate into degrading celebrations, complete with dancing and overdoses of alcohol.

On the eve of the feast, the Mother Superior sent Sister Martha to tell Brother Charles he must " absolutely " climb Mt. Tabor. Charles, already informed of what happened on such occasions, had no inclination to participate in anything so sacrilegious.

" But I don't know the way, " was his excuse.

" Oh, don't worry about that, " Sister Martha told him, " we'll give you directions. "

Charles bowed his head in obedient resignation, then fled to the chapel for prayer. But shortly afterward Sister Martha reappeared. " Here, good brother, " she said, " is the ladder you must use to climb Mt. Tabor, " and handed him a cardboard " ladder " on whose " steps " were inscribed, in the nuns' beautiful handwriting, the virtues one must practice in order to ascend the holy mount of God. By this time Sister Martha could no longer keep a straight face, and they both had a good laugh together.

He for his part thought the Sisters were merely making sport of him (not suspecting that they deliberately wanted to test him) and rejoiced at having created an image of himself as a simpleton. For he desired nothing more than to be mocked and despised, and had already found cause for unhappiness in the excessive deference these Sisters showed him. The fact was that the better the

Sisters got to know him and compared notes about him, the more they admired him. " Fortunately " Charles commented, " such is not the case in Nazareth. " Whenever he went, in his ragpicker's costume, to pick up the mail in town, there was never lacking some imp who would make insulting remarks or gestures of derision. On one occasion a group of youngsters chased him with stones. For Charles this was a day of rejoicing!

He had several of these " days of rejoicing, " each one of them a step downward, an act of extreme renunciation, an incident that elevated abnegation itself to the status of an ideal. A few of these concrete experiences are worth noting . . . .

Brother Charles of Jesus was his own barber, his rusty old scissors producing rather mediocre results. One day he knelt before a Carmelite priest who was visiting the convent, and asked the good father's blessing. The Carmelite noticed the botched-up barbering at once, and asked, " What's this, my friend? The seven-year itch? "

On another occasion the sister made him responsible for catching a jackal that had been " dining out " at the community's henhouse every night. A man who lived near the convent was asked if he would lend Charles a gun. When the good neighbor arrived with his weapon and saw what a ragged, mangy hired hand was going to use it, he decided that the fellow must be a worthless bum. Shaking his head in disgust, he sat down and for the next couple of hours explained the use of firearms. The sort of baby talk he used to make his point was the kind normally reserved for either children or morons.

To appreciate the rich irony of this, you must remember that Charles de Foucauld was the graduate of two military schools, a commissioned army officer who had seen combat in Algeria, and the man who had explored Morocco. This was the " pupil " who now meekly accepted such minute instructions, even accepting the barbs of his teacher's occasional sarcasm without wincing.

Then, as evening approached, he waited in ambush behind an olive tree, carrying out the instructions given him. He waited several hours without seeing hide nor hair of the jackal. Finally he laid the rifle across his knees and spent the rest of the night saying the rosary. When he returned to the convent at dawn, he learned that the jackal had enjoyed his usual menu of chicken á la henhouse, and he became the laughing-stock of all Nazareth.

On another occasion a visiting preacher was dining in the Poor Clares' reception room. It was just before Christmas, and the meal that Brother Charles was asked to serve him was exceptionally well cooked and plentiful, so that the visitor could not do full justice to it.

" Now it's your turn, " said the satiated guest as he got up from the table. " Sit down and eat a good meal for once. "

Charles saw in the man's eyes that he had the best of intentions, but that he also would enjoy the spectacle of a starved fellow creature making a gluttonous fool of himself. Not wanting to disappoint his audience (even though the sight of such food nauseated him) he decided to respond wholeheartedly to the invitation. Mumbling a little prayer of thanks, he attacked the table scraps full force, not quitting until every crumb was devoured. And throughout the whole performance he sought to display all the greediness of a starving man. Now, happy day, everyone would think him an absolute glutton! He had taken another step down on the ladder of humiliation.

One incident that brought him less joy than he could have hoped for occurred in the Sisters' courtyard, where he was sorting lentils. Two French religious passed by, and when he saw they were making sport of his " feminine " occupation, he blushed from ear to ear. But his blushes became the source of fresh humiliations, for he judged his own conduct inexcusable. " When Jesus lived here at Nazareth, would he have felt ashamed to be caught helping his mother? "

Thus he sought ardently, day after day, to be always a little more despised, a little more depreciated, that he might put his " self-life " to death, that he might become as much as possible one with Jesus in His disgrace and abjection.

On the feast of Pentecost he wrote in his journal a little memo to himself — a kind of prophecy that would later find its dramatic fulfillment: " Think of yourself as dying a martyr's death — stripped of every possession, thrown prostrate on the ground, naked, disfigured, covered with wounds and blood, the victim of a violent, disagreeable death . . . and wish that it might be today. "

What more could Brother Charles do that he had not already done during those first few months in Nazareth, to root out and eradicate the " old man " of which the Apostle Paul spoke? But he had still not succeeded in " robbing himself of self " to the extent he had hoped to. And so from the 5th to the 15th of November he went on retreat, maintaining absolute silence whether in the chapel or in his den, and giving himself completely to prayer and meditation.

As he " climbed the mountain of God " there was not one step of his climb that went unnoticed by the community of Poor Clares. Every fresh evidence of mortification, fasting, sleepless nights, or Charles' insatiable quest for derision in the eyes of fellow men was reported by the nuns who were in contact with him.

Mother Saint Michel engaged in a series of conversations with him in order to know him better, always from behind the grating and the impenetrable black curtain. Thus, without their ever laying eyes on each other, an extraordinary spiritual relationship began to grow between them, and with time it became ever stronger.

After a while Mother Saint Michel took into her confidence the Mother Superior of the Poor Clares convent in Jerusalem. Mother Elizabeth of Calvary, as she was called, also desired a first-hand acquaintance with Charles, and beginning around July, 1898, she summoned him to speak with her across the grating in her convent. In response to her questions he supplied her with a brief summary of his life to date.

Mother Elizabeth kept him at her convent for a while, concluding in time that " Nazareth was not mistaken about him. He is a real man of God, a saint in our very midst. " Then both she and Mother Saint Michel began a campaign of persuading him to become a priest.

As might be expected, Charles expressed an immediate and uncompromising opposition to any such idea. But day after day they hammered away at his defenses, repeatedly affirming that he had no right to bury the talents God had given him. At last the Mother Superior noticed with relief that his resistance was beginning to weaken. He still protested his unworthiness, still insisted that the priestly ministry was somehow incompatible with his vocation of abnegation, of " seeking the last place. " But now he was beginning to admit that perhaps he could become a priest, if in the process he might remain humble, poor, obscure, and despised.

And so, two years later, on June 9, 1901, after making a retreat at Our Lady of the Snows, his old Trappist community amid the chilly French hills of Vivarais, he allowed Monsignor Montéty of Viviers to lay his hands upon him, making him a priest. Mother Elizabeth of Calvary and Mother Saint Michel, God's instruments of the moment, had achieved what they set out to do. And Charles de Foucauld added another costume to his historic wardrobe — the black cassock of a priest.

Thus at the age of 42 another new life began for him. He was a priest in the diocese of Viviers, but from the very beginning of his priesthood he was granted an unconditional exemption from living in the diocese. But where would he live?

The choice was quite clear to him, because he had known for some time whither he was bound. " Already during the moments of solitude preceding my ordination, " he was to write later, " I had understood that my Nazareth-life, which seemed to be my vocation, did not require my residence in the Holy Land, much as I longed to live there, but among the very sickest of souls, amidst the most abandoned of human society. The divine banquet, which I could now dispense to others, was not something to give my relatives or my richer neighbors, but something with which to feed the lame and the blind, the poor and those who had no priest. "

Then what about Africa? Surely Africa, *his* Africa was such a place of need. After all, it was the Moslems of North Africa who, without realizing it, had awakened his longing for God. Now he must repay that debt a hundredfold by testifying, among them, to the true God. Memories that had lain dormant for eighteen years now rose clearly before his mind: " In the Moroccan interior, an area as large as France, there are ten million people without a single priest. In the Sahara, seven or eight times as large as France — and more heavily populated than was once thought — there are scarcely a dozen missionaries. Surely no population was ever more forsaken than this! "

He knew that the death of Sultan Moulay el Hasan had brought on an even more chaotic situation in Morocco than ever before, so that the entire Morocco-Algerian frontier was aflame with hostilities. Except for a few localities protected by French troops, there were not many Algerian oases near the Morocco border that were considered safe from the lightning attacks of Moorish marauders.

It was only farther south, in the very heart of the Sahara, that the French were making any real progress. There they had been occupying oases of the Saoura, whose population was a mixed race of Arab, Negro, and Jewish ancestry.

Charles knew that those oases were stepping stones to southern Morocco, and they became his goal. Meanwhile his life's dream — subdued but never extinguished within him — of founding his Congregation of the Little Brothers of Jesus, had a bearing on his latest decision: " On the Moroccan frontier we would like to found, not a Trappist community, nor a big, wealthy monastery, nor even an agricultural settlement, but a humble little hermitage where a few poor monks can live on a few fruits and vegetables they raise themselves. They would live in strict enclosure, doing penance and adoring the Blessed Sacrament, always in solitude and never preaching, but offering hospitality to all who ask, whether good or evil, friend or foe, Moslem or Christian . . . . You know the kind of community I want to build: a *zaouïa* of prayer and hospitality, from which will radiate the Gospel, truth, charity . . . Jesus. "

His use of the Arabic term *zaouïa*, usually applied to the headquarters of a Moslem religious fraternity, shows how much of Morocco was still in his blood.

Charles de Foucauld left for Algiers in September 1901, but his plans hit a snag almost at once. The Saoura was considered a military zone of operation, and civilians were not welcome. As for a priest setting foot there, nothing could be farther from the Governor General's mind. Nothing would be more likely, in his opinion, to make the Moslems more upset than they already were. And as for a priest such as Charles de Foucauld, who boldly announced plans to found a new congregation of religious on that very spot, there could only be one categorical answer — no!

Fortunately Charles discovered several of his old army buddies in Algiers, and learned that some of these were high-ranking officers in the North African Command. These erstwhile friends of his managed to iron out one difficulty after another, so that after a month's waiting he got traveling papers for the oases of Saoura, and more specifically Beni-Abbès, which, on the basis of information at his disposal, seemed his most appropriate base of operations, because 1) it comprised several villages of indigenous Saharans; 2) a French garrison was stationed there; 3) no other priests lived around there; and 4) it was the oasis closest to southern Morocco.

At this point Charles de Foucauld adopted the next in his almost endless series of distinctive costumes this time the garb of Saharan natives: a white *gandourah* and a lightweight, white *cheche.* Two special badges were added to this basic costume: a large rosary that hung from his sash, and on the bib of his *gandourah* a large red heart surmounted with a red cross.

An ancient railway train transported him jauntily to within a few miles of Figuig, an especially troubled oasis. From there the only means of access to Beni-Abbès was a little trail that skirted the edge of Morocco.

Charles de Foucauld had intended to proceed from here on foot, but someone spoiled his plans: " Around here, we don't just come and go as we please. You will have to go by horseback, *monsieur l'Abbé!* "

So he obtained a horse and was escorted to his destination by a lieutenant (returning from leave) and a group of native soldiery.

Passing over his trip through the Saharan dunes, we find him at the gates of Beni-Abbès. Here the stark highlands of the desert loom suddenly into view beyond the arid moonscape of the plains. From the hills there flows a shiny ribbon of water, the Wadi Saoura, giving life to a jungle of seven to eight thousand green-crested palms, from whose midst a massive yellow promontory erupts into the heavens.

If Charles de Foucauld entertained any notions of living more obscurely in the Sahara than he had at Nazareth, he was soon to be disillusioned. Captain Regnault, commanding officer of the local garrison, wined and dined him in the presence of all his junior officers, and numerous prominent citizens of the three native villages — Negroes and Berbers, representing 1,500 inhabitants — left their orchards and lush gardens to go and pay their respects to him. His reputation — as a brilliant Hussar, a courageous army officer, and an intrepid explorer of Morocco — had preceded him by several days. As he reached out to take a forest of hands, he introduced himself as " Brother Charles of Jesus. " But they already gave him a name before his arrival, as soon as they received news of his coming. The French were calling him " Father Foucauld " and expected him to live on the post. The Arabs christened him the " *marabout* of the red heart " and would not hear of his staying anywhere except in the villages.

The military camp was austere enough for him, but there were too many comforts available for his taste; and life in the villages was too colorful for Brother Charles. His home must be neither in camp nor village, but alone in the desert with God. At the same time he must be close enough to be accessible to anyone who needed him. And since this was the Morocco-Algerian frontier, his most appropriate location would be somewhere on the line of demarkation between the French and the Arabs, between Christian and Moslem.

About half a mile from Beni-Abbès his explorations brought him to an extensive plateau, devoid of vegetation, which fell away suddenly into a deep ravine. He descended its steep incline into the spooky silence of that sunburned rock chamber, but stopped halfway to the bottom. From there all he could see was an abundance of nothing. Neither fortress towers nor palm fronds were visible from here — only desolate sand dunes funneling an empty sky. At the bottom of the depression Charles could make out a clump of sickly-looking brambles — indicating there had been some wells here once. Perfect! Here was where his hermitage would be — halfway down the slope of this Dante-style inferno.

" To receive the grace of God, " he wrote that evening to a Trappist friend, " you must go to a desert place and stay awhile. There you can be emptied and unburdened of everything that does not pertain to God. There the house of your soul is swept clean to make room for God alone to dwell. The Israelites had to pass through the desert.

Moses lived there before he was commissioned for his lifework. St. Paul, St. John Chrysostom — both of them served apprenticeship in the desert . . . . Here is an occasion of grace, a condition through which every soul ought to pass, if it is to bear fruit. We need this silence, this absence of every creature, so that God can build his hermitage within us, and create a spiritual life within us . . . . Consider also St. John the Baptist and Our Lord Himself — He who had no need of the desert, but dwelt there nevertheless, as an example to us. "

He wrote also to Cousin Marie de Bondy, because he needed money: a thousand francs to purchase the necessary acreage of desert crater from the *caid of* Beni-Abbès. Along that tortured slope he hoped to find a spot where he could make a little garden grow. The money arrived, and Charles went to work. He put up his little hermitage, spaded his garden, reactivated the old wells, and planted a few palms and olive trees. He soon realized, however, that all this was more than a one-man job. Captain Regnault, apparently suspecting this, sent some soldiers over to help him lay the bricks.

The first project to be completed was the chapel. But what a chapel! Not even the poorest little church in the remotest valley of Europe could compare with it for modesty. Except for the little wooden cross on the roof, it was indistinguishable from the Arab huts to be found in nearby villages, and internally it differed in no way from the other five rooms being built.

Of these, one would serve as a cell for Brother Charles, two would be guest rooms, and the other two were for the companions he hoped would join him, for in his craving to be united with others in charity, he was always hoping for the day when he would have followers to share his way of life.

A very crude piece of construction, that little chapel, but it was still the Lord's house, and Charles had nothing but enthusiasm when he described it to Cousin Marie: " The interior of the chapel is coated with a ceramic paste, kind of a dark gray in color, or maybe we should call it a very dark shade of pearl — sort of a grayish black, I mean. It's a very becoming color, anyway. The room is four meters high. The ceiling, or roof actually, is horizontal, and thatched with large palm fronds. A little on the rustic side, rather poor, but harmonious and attractive, nevertheless. To hold up the roof there are four vertical pillars made from the trunks of palm trees. They increase the rustic effect and make a nice setting for the altar. On the Gospel side I have hung a kerosene lamp that serves as a night light and also to illuminate the altar. I brought the white wood altar with me from Our Lady of the Snows, where I had it made according to my own specifications. Actually it's a board, dismountable, resting on square legs, and a tabernacle right in the middle. The cross is of ebony, covered with leather, a very lovely thing given me by the Mother Superior of the Jerusalem Poor Clares. From the ceiling a canopy hangs down in the shape of a tent. It's made of a very impermeable dark green silk, and this protects the altar and its vestments in case of rain. Actually the roof is more of a shelter against the sun than against the rain. The floor is covered with a layer of red sand ten centimeters thick. Sand is one thing they have a good supply of in this country! "

On the first of December, 1901, Charles de Foucauld celebrated Mass there for the first time. " Anyone who didn't assist at that Mass, " says an old soldier who served as acolyte, "doesn't know what a real Mass is. When Father Foucauld recited the *Domine, non sum dignus*, there wasn't a dry eye among those present. "

God Calls from the Southeast

In late summer, 1901, when Charles de Foucauld was leaving France for Africa — no longer as a soldier or explorer but as a priest — he found the Arabic terminology very useful to him in describing his dream of the future. You will remember that he had once written, " We want to inaugurate on the Moroccan frontier . . . a *zaouïa* of prayer and hospitality. " And this *zaouïa*, as has been mentioned, means for Moslems a place where the members of a religious fraternity meet and live together.

With his own hands he built the little group of Algerian-style huts, halfway down the sun-filled slope of that Saharan crater near the Beni-Abbés oasis. But by early spring of 1902 he had to recognize one stubborn fact: no Little Brothers of Jesus had shown up to occupy those two little rooms prepared for them, and there they remained, idle and empty. So out of his stock of Arabic words he brought a different term to describe his new hermitage. The weird little assembly of native-style huts was hereafter to be known as " the *khaoua* of the Sacred Heart, " and by *khaoua* he meant a " house of brotherhood " where everyone that passed by on a journey was to be treated as a brother.

We doubt if *khaoua* sounded as delightful to his ears as *zaouïa*, because he still awaited the arrival of someone who would settle down there and live in perfect unity of spirit with him in Christ. Then the " hermit's hostel " could become the " community hostel " he had hoped to found.

He never resigned himself to this solitude but continued to do all he could to call others as co-laborers in what he considered the most barren corner of the Lord's vineyard. On one occasion he wrote to his former Trappist Superiors at Our Lady of the Snows in France, and also to the Algerian community at Staouëli, inquiring if there might not be some novice there who would like to live the same life as he. But the two abbots did not even put the question to their novices. Fearing that Charles' insatiable craving for penance and abnegation could have adverse consequences in the lives of anyone who might follow him, they felt it necessary to answer him with a very regretful " no. " One of the good abbots remarked at the time: " The only thing that puzzles me about Father Foucauld is that he doesn't perform any miracles. I have never known another real-life saint like this. He is the kind you normally just read about in books. However, the penances he performs are such that I am afraid they would kill any novice in a very short time. I would even say that the *spiritual* discipline he imposes on himself — and would seek to impose on his disciples — is something practically superhuman, and would drive anyone else crazy, even before the rigorous penances had destroyed his physical health. "

Around his hermitage Charles de Foucauld erected a kind of wall or barricade, which was nothing but a long, low line of rocks piled up, and scarcely distinguishable from the other rocks in that part of the desert ravine. Beyond this wall Charles pledged himself never to go except in dire emergencies. To him it was an added security measure that accentuated his vow of monastic enclosure and reinforced the barrier, already formed by the desert, between him and the oasis. But it was a one-way boundary that kept him in, but kept no " outsider " out, for it was easy to climb over. And so, for everyone else — French soldiers or officers, Arabs or Berbers, local chieftain or common beggar, Christian or Moslem, sick people or slaves — and especially for the slaves — this boundary had no real meaning, indeed did not really exist at all.

A report submitted to Algiers at that time by Captain Regnault, commander of the French outpost at Beni-Abbès, says, " In order to insure a life of monastic seclusion, the reverend Father Foucauld has set up on the ground around his living quarters a barrier beyond which he never passes. With the help of some natives whom he recompensed out of his own pocket, he has planted some barley on the slope to the east of his hermitage. And he has excavated some wells in order to provide the necessary irrigation. He lives on dates and some bread furnished him by the local administration. He uses his own money to buy the wheat, barley, and dates that he distributes to the poor. Despite repeated admonitions from the garrison authorities, he refuses to make any changes in his diet. When vegetables are given him for making soup, he will sooner or later give them to the poor or to some guest who has spent the night in his home. The poor of Saoura regard Father Foucauld with the deepest respect. His generosity and his abnegation are qualities they reverence and admire. "

We have also some comments that Charles himself made in a letter to Monsignor Guérin of the White Fathers, who as Apostolic Prefect of Ghardaïa exercised spiritual authority over all the Catholics in those regions of the Sahara administered from Algiers. " To have an exact idea of my life, " he wrote, " you have to realize that someone knocks on my door at least ten times every hour of the day — poor people, sick people, travelers who need a place for the night. "

Christians came to assist at his Mass and pray with him — a priest of Christ. Moslems came to discuss the things of God with this " *marabout* of the red heart.* " Beggars came to ask for food or clothes from the poorest white man in all the Sahara. Slaves fled to him for protection — yet the protector was the most defenseless, unprotected Frenchman in all Algeria. All that was sent him from the military post in Beni-Abbès was distributed at once to the poor, as was everything that he bought — barley, dates, yard goods, whatever. And if a poor person needed lodging, the hermitage was always open to him.

Despite all this, he decided during a retreat that he was still not practicing enough hospitality, and determined that from now on he would launder his guest's clothes, make their beds, straighten up their rooms, do their patching and mending, and serve them food and water with his own hands. Thus he would do " everything of a servile nature, and in this way be like Jesus, who was among the Apostles as one who served. "

But the " poorest of the poor " were the Negro slaves, and Charles soon learned that, for these, even such " services " only scratched the surface of their need.

He had not been in Beni-Abbès more than a few days before he was confronted head on with the frightening facts of the case. At that time the European press chose to ignore the problem, or even denied its existence. But the fact of the matter was that in the Sahara, in the 1,901st year of the grace of our Lord, the slave traffic was still going strong, and quite openly! The buying and selling of human beings was being carried on in the full light of day, and the flesh merchants did their work unmolested and unpunished. In French metropolitan areas, fine words like equality, fraternity, and liberty were freely bandied, but here at the far edge of Algeria the French winked at the grisly slave traffic — or more often closed both eyes — because they wanted to avoid trouble with the oasis officials and tribal chiefs, who owned the majority of the slaves.

These unfortunates were given the most burdensome tasks to perform, above all to draw water from the wells in pitchers, often without the benefit of pulleys. From morn to evening they labored to irrigate the palm trees. If they slowed up in their work, they would feel the skin-peeling lash on their ebony backs. If they ran away, they would be hunted down with rifles, like wild animals. If any were ever caught alive, the tendons of their feet would be cut, so that they would never be able to run again. " Slaves, " said Charles de Foucauld, " receive nothing for their work, which means they can never purchase their own freedom. Their material misery is bad enough, but morally they are even worse off. They are almost devoid of religious faith, and their lives are lived out in an atmosphere of hatred and desperation. "

He, perhaps more than anyone, understood the subhumanity of their condition and the anguish burning within their souls. Every day, at least a score of slaves would climb over his wall of enclosure and take refuge in his *khaoua*. And for each one there was always a word of charity that somehow quieted their hearts. He would always come up with a piece of bread, a little something to wear, and an avalanche of kindness. But when he noticed that all who came, without exception, threw themselves at his feet and begged with heartbreaking sobs to be set free, then more and more he began to feel that what these wretched souls needed was not just kindness, not just comforting words or bread or clothes, but freedom. But where do you dig up the resources to buy freedom for a vast horde of slaves? And every day the situation seemed to grow more hopeless.

Charles de Foucauld had a fairly predictable income. His cousin Marie de Bondy provided from her funds for the upkeep of the chapel, while every month the officers and enlisted men of the Beni-Abbès military base took up a collection for him, usually amounting to 40 or 50 francs. Fifty francs come every month from his cousin Catherine de Flavigny, and 20 more from his sister Marie de Blic. Altogether, then, he received 110-120 francs per month, and every bit of it went to the poor.

This was all he could give, and using this to help the multitudes of the desert's dispossessed, the majority of the population, was like trying to irrigate the whole Sahara with a drop of water.

But even then he managed to buy freedom for seven slaves. The first of these was a nomad whom slave traders had captured during a raid. He returned to his own tribe as soon as he was free. A second and third disappeared at once and were never heard of again. The fourth and fifth were children, the youngest a three-year-old, whom he

baptized and named Abd Jesus (Servant of Jesus).
These two he sent to an orphanage run by the
White Fathers. The sixth to be ransomed was a
very old Negro woman who died in the hermitage
just a few days after her liberation. Before death
she asked for baptism, and he christened her
" Marie. " (These two baptisms, Marie and Abd
Jesus, seem to have been the only two he ever
performed. He was not the " pastor " of Beni-
Abbès, nor did he consider himself a " missionary "
— a term that normally implies a preaching
ministry — for he felt called to this place only
for the sake of living, in silence, the life the Son
of God lived at Nazareth. But this in itself proved
to be a " testimony, " regardless of his intentions.)

The seventh slave that he freed was a boy
named Paul Embarek, who after he grew bigger
tried on several occasions to leave his benefactor
and live his own life. But he always came back,
defeated by the hardships he encountered, and at
last he became a faithful companion, remaining
with Charles until the very moment of his death.

But this handful of liberations did not go
unnoticed. The news spread like the wind to every
oasis of the Saoura, and from all that region the
unfortunates began a freedom march, converging
on the " *khaoua* of the Sacred Heart. "

Of course the slaveowners of every local tribe
were alarmed by all this, and registered vigorous
protests with the occupation officials in Beni-Abbès.

This apprehension could not help rubbing off on the garrison officers, who were threatened both by the reactions of the native chieftains and by the disapproval of their home government. For while the Saharan oases were being agitated by the winds of " liberation, " the monsoons of freemasonry were whipping up anticlerical gales in France, and Premier Combes, bent on the destruction of religious Orders in general, had no soft spot in his heart for " meddling priests. "

So for this reason the military authorities counseled Charles to proceed with maximum prudence. But for Charles de Foucauld the dictates of " prudence " were no match for the horrors of the slave trade that paraded before his eyes every day, and when he reacted it was with the totality of his being.

He began by writing to a cousin in Paris, Captain de Castries, whom he knew to be influential in the Ministry of Native Affairs and had good " connections " with the more prominent members of the National Assembly. He also wrote to Monsignor Guérin, who represented the authority of the Church in those parts: " The slave traffic here is a nasty business, and as long as we French permit it to exist, even help it along, then we are making fools of ourselves . . . . The natives know we officially condemn slaveholding, that we don't permit it among our own people . . . , so when they see us letting them get away with it, then they say we are yellow, that we are afraid of them, and they have every right to make fun of us . . . . No one in the world has any right to keep these unfortunates in chains, when God has created them every bit as free as ourselves. When we permit their so-called owners to hold them against their will, when we help find those who escaped, when we betray those who appeal to the French authorities for justice and protection and we take them back to their masters, then we are robbing them of their most precious possession . . . . We have no right to play the part of bloodhounds or stone-faced sentinels in the face of such wickedness; we must cry out in protest! There is no other remedy for this abomination, this miscarriage of justice, except to set these people free. Search the world over and you will find no justification, political or economic, for such immorality, such iniquity! "

We are not at all sure how much Monsignor Guérin was able to accomplish, threatened as he was by the stormclouds of anticlericalism that hung over France. Nor do we have any idea how effective his cousin was in manipulating the machinery of the State. But we do know that Charles de Foucauld did his part, and did it fully. And judging by what happened at Beni-Abbès and its sister oases, it seems safe to say that Captain Regnault took a stand locally against slavery, regardless (sometimes in spite) of what Paris and Algiers felt about it.

In fact, after Charles had been in Beni-Abbès for three years, he was able to write to Captain de Castries that " of their own accord our colonial authorities have taken measures to suppress slavery: not all at once — that would be unwise — but gradually, so that in a short time there will be no more slaves here. It can now actually be said that real slavery, understood in its classical sense, no longer exists. Slave traffic is strictly forbidden, those still in slavery cannot change owners, and if they are not treated well they can be set free. Thus a big step has already been taken. "

While Charles de Foucauld was waging his war on slavery, some other things were going on, about which we have said very little so far. But these events are also woven into the dramatic fabric of his life, and we will need to say something about them.

It was while Charles was writing the first rough draft of a new monastic rule that the political situation in the Sahara took a turn for the worse. The rule he was drafting, we might mention, was for the Little Sisters of Jesus. The Little Brothers of Jesus still remained an unfulfilled dream, but this did not prevent the dreamer from visualizing some other small communities, made up of women, who would also live together " the life of Nazareth " in various mission fields.

But at the very moment when he was most engrossed in this, in July 1903, to be exact, the Moroccan guerrillas, not content with their usual small-scale raids on this or that oasis, tried something more spectacular right outside the gates of Beni-Abbès. About 200 Moroccans swooped down on a detachment of 50 Algerian riflemen and killed 22 of them. Captain Regnault immediately ordered a punitive expedition. About 80 camel riders and horsemen set up an ambush along the route they knew the Moroccans would be taking home, cutting off their retreat and putting about twenty of them out of commission.

The oasis of Beni-Abbès honored Captain Regnault as a hero, but Sheriff Moulay Mustafa replied by declaring a holy war. Marching at the head of 4,000 Berbers, accompanied by women and children (about 9,000 souls) and their flocks and herds of camels, donkeys, and goats, he moved against the oases of Saoura. Within the space of a few hours Taghit, the most populated and therefore the best fortified of these oases, was overrun with terrified refugees from the smaller oases nearby, which because of their size were more difficult to defend. In the midst of the unbelievable disorder that ensued, Captain Susbielle, commanding officer at Taghit and one of Charles' former comrades in arms, had scarcely time to throw together some sort of defense. All he could actually rely on were two 80 mm. cannon and a total of 470 fighting men.

The human tidal wave of Moulay Mustafa headed straight through the sand dunes for Taghit, inspiring some of the superstitious fear the Biblical pagans must have felt when the children of Israel began the conquest of Canaan. Three days of continual attacks were made, the first a mass assault, afterwards a series of scattered forays. But Taghit did not fall, and the Sheriff was finally forced to retreat toward the Moroccan border, leaving 1,200 dead on the battlefield.

But during the period of retreat, two hundred Moorish warriors, passing near El Moungar, ran onto a hundred French legionnaires escorting a caravan, and massacred them. By the time Captain Susbielle could come to their rescue, all he could do was to bury the dead in the sands of the Sahara, then gather up the 49 wounded and take them back to Taghit.

News of the battle reached Beni-Abbès, creating panic in the three villages of the oasis. Charles de Foucauld realized at once that in the present circumstances he would have to disregard the wall around his hermitage. His place, he decided, was beside the 49 wounded men, because in that moment they were his most needy brothers. He went to the fort and requested a horse to ride and permission to go to Taghit.

" You're crazy, " the garrison officers told him, but they gave him a horse. Equipped with spurs and wrapped in a *burnous,* he disappeared at full gallop over the sandy horizon.

" He'll make it, " said Captain Regnault, replying to the reproving glances that seemed about to charge him with murdering the hermit of the Sacred Heart. " Yes, he'll get through. I'm telling you this because he would be too modest to say it himself, but that man could travel unarmed across the whole country even if it were convulsed by rebellion, and no one would harm a hair on his

117

head. He is considered sacred! " And the Captain was right. He did get through.

When Captain Susbielle met him coming out from his first session with the wounded, he knew very well that his men, all hardened veterans of the Foreign Legion, went more for tobacco than they did for religion, so that there was a little sarcasm in his voice when he asked: " Well, my dear Padre, and how did you make out? Did your new flock give you a suitable reception? "

" Oh well, " answered Charles de Foucauld, his tiny eyes twinkling, " It takes time to get acquainted, but I'm sure we will. At the moment I'm just happy I can be here with them. "

He stayed three weeks, but " it didn't take long for him to win them all over with his kindness, his concern for them at every moment, his bouyant spirits, " wrote Captain Susbielle, looking back on it all. " When he entered their room, they would vie with each other for the privilege of having him come to this or that man's bed first, and then the fortunate party would try to keep him there as long as he could, over the protests of the others. He never tired of writing letters for them, cheering them up, talking with them in a low voice. Little by little he began speaking to them of God and religion. I remember one man in particular. He was of German ancestry, and had led a troubled life. He had a bad wound in his chest and the doctor didn't expect him to live. At first he gave the Padre a hard time, but after a day or two he could hardly bear to have him leave. And, along with all his comrades, he eventually made his Confession and received Communion. "

After what had happened at Taghit and El Moungar, Paris decided a strong hand was needed, and General Lyautey, another of Charles' old comrades, was sent to take over command. They had been Hussars together at Sezanne and riflemen together during the campaign of 1881.

Lyautey happened to be assuming his new responsibilities at his headquarters in Aïn Sefra just as Charles was passing through on his return from Taghit.

" He stayed with me three days, " writes the General, " very graciously accepting my hospitality and dining at my table. Many of those who sat at the table with us were people you know: Major Henrys, Captain Beriau, Captain Poemyrau, and others. These were all the jolliest sort of fellows, full of fun. We did not hesitate, of course, to discuss his scientific work in Morocco and some of the problems of Africa. But, as you well know, we are soldiers and not quite up to dwelling only on serious topics for three days in a row. As we kept jumping from one subject to another, more than once we forgot for a while that this was Father Foucauld and not the Lieutenant Foucauld we had known. But he never seemed the least bit embarrassed, and he never refused to taste the champagne we set before him. I can still see him asking Poemyrau to play a certain tune on the piano. To myself I said: *He may be a saint, all right, but at the same time he is not afraid to live it up with his old buddies.*

"But he had his own way of living it up! Just after he started on his way again, I got a telegram from Algiers tipping me off that within an hour a group of highly recommended tourists would be stopping off with us. I called an orderly and told him to get Father Foucauld's room straightened up right away. 'But, *mon général,* there is no need to straighten anything up, because nothing was ever disturbed. He slept all three nights on the ground, wrapped up in his *burnous.*'

"See what I mean? Only then did it dawn on me how much courtesy and self-control he had been practicing, trying to ensure that his presence at our table would not make anyone uncomfortable, or what an austerity he had imposed on his conscience in order to make this temporary and unwelcome exception to his own Rule. "

A few weeks later, General Lyautey had to go to Beni-Abbès, at a moment when traveling was especially dangerous, and he only got through by using a heavy escort and often forcing his way through with the aid of rifle fire.

He looked up Charles de Foucauld at once, and was informed that the priest was leaving next day on a trip to Algiers.

"Tomorrow? Are you kidding? You'll have to wait two or three days to leave here. Wait and go north with me. After all, we can't furnish an escort just for you. "

Charles replied that he had his responsibilities and intended to discharge them. Lyautey became irritated.

Then Captain Regnault intervened. " But, *mon général,* did it ever occur to you that Father Foucauld needs no escort. He could pass through the middle of any band of guerrillas in this whole desert and not be shot at. When a rider meets him in the desert, he gets off his horse, throws himself on the ground, kisses the folds of his *burnous,* and asks him for a blessing. So let him go. "

" It was thus revealed to me, " the General wrote afterward, " what power this man possessed, for among Moslems all over the Sahara he was respected as a true *marabout.* "

Charles went back to his *khaoua* of the Sacred Heart and resumed his " life of Nazareth. " He was beginning work on " The Gospel for Poor Negroes of the Sahara " — just in case someday one would ask for something besides dates and cereal — when word reached him of new violence in Africa. The latest was that El Hoggar was having a revolution, and every indication was that France would take advantage of the occasion to extend her sphere of influence.

El Hoggar, the arid heart of the Sahara, land of endless thirst and fear; a frozen, silent typhoon of jagged lava projecting its red, black, and green volcanic peaks upward to ten thousand feet....

El Hoggar, home of the Touareg, blue-veiled camel riders who plummeted down upon caravans, the scourge of the desert, plundering and destroying as they went.

One day a letter arrived for Charles from In Salah, largest of the French-held oases in southern Algeria, bordering on the Hoggar country. It was from General Laperrine, commander of the Oasis Territory. Good old Laperrine, Charles' schoolmate at St. Cyr, his comrade in arms in the Fourth African Regiment! He made passing reference to the storm brewing in southern skies, but his main subject was the Touareg.

The letter hit Charles de Foucauld like a bolt of lightning. For years now he had lived in his *khaoua* with eyes and ears trained on the west, toward Morocco. But at this moment he saw Christ beckoning him along a trail that led in the opposite direction. The Lord's footsteps pointed to the southeast, to the Touareg, a people hidden away in the rocky desert where the name of Christ had never been heard. And he alone could go to them, because he was the only priest in the whole world, at the moment, who could be authorized to enter the Hoggar.

And so, once more, he forsook everything. He had left a life of amorous adventures to become an adventurer for science. He had deserted a career of exploring to enter La Trappe. He had turned his back on the Trappists for a hermitage in Nazareth, and then forsook the hermitage to found his House of Brotherhood or Fraternity, at Beni-Abbès.

Now, for the last time, he climbed over the pile of rocks that had served as his enclosure, in order to follow the call of God ever deeper into the desert's heart, forever renouncing " his " Morocco in favor of the untamed terrors of El Hoggar.

His heart almost failed him. " My whole nature shrinks back unbelievably from such a prospect. I rebel — and then feel ashamed at my rebellion — against the thought of leaving Beni-Abbès, and the peace to be found here at the foot of the altar, in order to launch out adventurously on travels for which I feel at the moment only an unspeakable horror. "

But how could one refuse the call? " I have received an invitation, I am expected .... The more I travel, the more natives I will meet and the better I will be known by them. "

And at once he wrote down a plan of procedure: " Establish residence among the Touareg, as near the heart of their land as possible. Pray, study their language and translate the Holy Gospel. Enter into contact with the Touareg. Abandon monastic seclusion. Every year go north to make my Confession, administer sacraments at outposts along route. Speak to natives about God, wherever I travel. "

And when his new adventure began, early in 1904, he recalled what he had written just a few months earlier: " Every moment let me live as though I were to die this evening, a martyr .... Let me prepare myself unceasingly for martyrdom, that I may receive it without the least thought of self-defense, even as the Lamb of God was defenseless. "

And perhaps he was aware, even then, how prophetic those words would prove to be.

A Knock at the Door

December 1, 1916. The chill-laden evening shadows were beginning to submerge the bare rocks of the Tamanrasset Plateau in the Hoggar, first submerging the deep mountain canyons, but eventually reaching the ramparts of the little stockade, a squat, angular structure built of homemade red bricks.

There was a tower at each of the four corners of the red-brick stockade, and a deep ditch surrounded it. A little bridge spanned the moat, leading to the castle's only entrance, low and protected by a series of baffles. The door opened onto a passageway (scarcely more than a cleft in the wall) and in the process of getting through this, a visitor had to climb over a sort of barrier, practically bending double to avoid bumping his skull on an overhead beam. One also had to pass two bolted doors to clear the passageway and enter an inner court. In the center of the inner cloister were a little pond and a baking oven, and a series of narrow doorways led to rudely furnished rooms.

Charles de Foucauld was occupying one of these cells that evening, and had begun writing some letters. He was all alone within the stockade walls. Even Paul Embarek, the slave he had freed at Beni-Abbès, had left for the Harratin village about a half mile away to spend the night with his wife and children in the little hut they called home.

Charles knew he would be getting a visit from Bou Aicha and Boudjema ben Brahim, two camel riders who delivered mail for him, and so, after writing a letter to his old friend General Laperrine and his sister Marie de Blic, he bent once more over the packing case that served him as a table, and by the feeble light of a little candle stub tried to finish a letter to his cousin Marie de Bondy: " The negation of our own selves is the most powerful means we have at our disposal if we would unite ourselves with Jesus and do good to other souls. "

At this moment someone knocked at the door. He went out into the courtyard and shouted into the dark passageway, " Who is it? "

" It's the mailman, " said the familiar voice of El Madani, a Harratin whom he had fed and looked after a number of times.

Charles picked his way through the corridor and opened the door . . . .

At the time of the above incident, Charles de Foucauld had been living in the Hoggar for 13 years, ever since that distant January of 1904 when, joining a military column, he and Paul Embarek had left the hermitage of Beni-Abbès — with the portable chapel loaded on the back of a donkey and a smaller burro trotting along behind, carrying with him only a few provisions and an extra pair of foot wraps, to begin the long trek southward that led among bare black hills. They were a month traveling, on foot, and relentlessly escorted by a swarm of flies. Every few hours they would see, among the endless bare rocks, a stunted little cactus plant. Every few days they would see, floating on the horizon, a little green oasis that turned out to be a mirage. Every week or so, they would come to a real oasis, and there Father Foucauld would abandon himself to a period of acquaintance with those who lived there, distributing to the very poorest people a few coins from his slender purse, or some provisions from his dwindling supply.

They passed through a fantastic region that was like a vast garden of rock crystal — unpredictable shapes, of a thousand different shades of color, overshadowed by great pink cliffs, beneath a sky (it was winter) that resembled clear quartz — finally arriving at In Salah and General Headquarters of the French Territory of the Oases.

Here General Laperrine brought Charles up on the news: of the six Touareg federations, three had shown themselves ready to accept French suzerainty: the Kel-Ahaggar in El Hoggar, the Taïtoq of Ahnet, and the Iforass of Adrar. Laperrine, logically enough, was planning to leave as soon as possible for a long trip through the Hoggar, the Ahnet, and the Adrar, in order to speed up the process and obtain the three tribes' complete surrender to France.

"And you, you old hermit, are you coming with us? "

"Do you think I'd stay behind, you old soldier? "

Charles, for his part, could not imagine a more favorable opportunity than this one would be to penetrate the mysterious depths of the Sahara — where God was calling him to live the life of Nazareth, but outside the enclosure.

In order to make the best of the time that would elapse while the big expedition was being equipped for travel, he headed at once, on his own, for the oasis of Akabli, where he had been told the Touareg caravans often stopped.

And at Akabli, in February 1904, he saw them for the first time. Scattered among the usual little groupings of arrogant Arabs all wrapped up in their white *burnouses,* the Touareg stood out in bold relief. Tall in stature, they stood very erect, maintained a majestic silence, and moved about with feline agility. The blue veils they used to cover their faces extended all the way to their feet, and over the tops of their veils, huge black eyes snapped with fierceness. The skin of their faces was bronze in color, stained with the same blue dye with which they colored their clothes.

So these were the blue-veiled warriors! In direct contrast to Arab custom, the men kept their faces covered, while the women went about unveiled — and they were attractive women, exquisitely charming and quick-witted, enjoying a freedom unknown to their Arab sisters. Here and there throughout the oasis, next to their dozing camels, the Touareg pitched their long, low tents of red leather, the north and south ends always left open for ventilation.

Beginning the day of his arrival, Charles de Foucauld went from one tent to another, offering his friendship to each one. In a week's time he had not only made many friends but had digested quite a bit of the Touareg vocabulary. Yet he knew from the start that he must thoroughly master this language if he was to communicate the will of the Most High to them with any effectiveness.

So he hired a Touareg as his teacher and was soon translating and composing in Tamashek, as the language is called, using the system of writing known as Tifinar. It is an extraordinarily pure, strictly African language, as distinguished from Arabic, which is of Asian origin. It is not the impoverished language of an uncultured people, but possesses a complex grammar and a rich vocabulary.

Three weeks after his arrival in the Akabli oasis, Charles saw the party of General Laperrine approaching over the sand dunes. The general was

129

stopping to pick him up on his way south, destination Timbuktu, which was " deep south " in Saharan geography. Laperrine, with his colonial ambitions, wanted to exploit his extensive tour to the full, not only to accept the surrender of the Touareg tribes but also to show the direct relationship there would hereafter be between Algeria and the Sudan.

As the caravan advanced slowly into the Hoggar, Charles de Foucauld spoke with everyone he met, visited every oasis, entered every encampment, observed everything with that same acuteness that had characterized his exploration of forbidden Morocco, many years earlier.

He discovered that the Touareg people of El Hoggar were divided into three castes. First there were *the nobles,* of which the Ken Rela clan was apparently the most illustrious, since the Amenokal, or supreme ruler of the Hoggar, was always chosen from their ranks. The reigning Amenokal at the time was Moussa, who continued to let the French believe he was ready to submit to their yoke. But in fact, although he knew Laperrine was traveling through his territory, he never showed up to discuss the terms of a treaty.

Secondly, there were *the vassals.* These, like the nobles, carried arms and owned goats and camels. They were chiefly a warrior caste. The third and most numerous caste, *the plebeians,* made their living by raising livestock and engaging in commerce.

130

After covering the entire Hoggar without making any treaty, they penetrated the Adrar, domain of the Iforass Touareg, who, by contrast, came to terms at once. Laperrine's next destination was Timiaouine, on the road to Timbuktu, but as he went his way, he was met by an armed patrol, in attack formation, obviously with intentions of blocking his further progress. The ridiculous thing about the whole situation was that this patrol blocking his way was commanded by French officers from Niger.

The Southern Sahara authorities, it turned out, were rather peeved by Laperrine's interference in affairs normally considered part of *their* responsibility. They were also unhappy to learn that he, not they, had made the treaty with the Iforass, and now they were bent on getting even by embarrassing him, and preventing him from preceeding to Timbuktu.

Laperrine would most certainly have fought back with arms, if Father Foucauld had not said just the right thing at the right moment. The General found strength to give in to his opponent's wrath, and the caravan turned back, heading instead for the Ahnet region, home of the Taïtoq, another Touareg tribe. This group also swore allegiance to France.

At last the moment came for Laperrine to go back to In Salah and leave Charles de Foucauld alone in his new " enclosure, " whose only boundaries were the limts of the desert itself.

Charles returned to the Hoggar and wandered for five months from one encampment to another, staying only a day or so in one spot, continually making new friendships in this unboundaried domain of the nomads. Every day he celebrated Mass, Paul Embarek acting as server. He spent time in prayer and meditation, spoke with as many of the Touareg as he could, lent a helping hand when needed, and despite his constant movement from place to place, he found time and strength to complete his translation of the Gospels into Tamashek. Perhaps someday there would be Touaregs who would want to read that translation. Would he ever live to see it? Meanwhile the Hoggar was his " new world, " and here he would have " pitched his tent forever. "

But Laperrine was rather worried about this commitment, and felt uneasy about Charles' safety, for which he had assumed personal responsibility. For although the scattered Iforass and Taïtoq tribes had surrendered, there was still Moussa, Amenokal of the Hoggar, who had not formally done so. And who could know what he was hatching up for the future? It would be better to wait and get in touch with the Amenokal himself, if at all possible, and ask his permission to settle among the Touareg. And so for the moment it would be better not to make any definite commitments, etc., etc.

In obedience to his friend's suggestions, Charles withdrew to In Salah, continuing on to Ghardaïa, where one of the White Fathers heard his confession and where he counseled with Monsignor Guérin, his religious superior. At the time he was only 46 years old, but was so thin and emaciated that he appeared to be 60. In ten months he had traveled over 3,000 miles on foot!

Proceeding to Beni-Abbès, site of his former *khaoua* of the Sacred Heart, he began to think that perhaps he should divide his time between the Touareg and the Arabs and French of the Saoura.

But he was only four months in Beni-Abbès. In May, 1905, Captain Dinaux had to provide escort for an expedition to the Hoggar, the party consisting of a journalist, a geologist, a historian, and an inspector of communications. Charles took advantage of this opportunity to return to the South, taking along Paul Embarek.

It was a frightening trip, conducted in the scorching heat of a Saharan summer. " After two hours on foot in the early morning hours, " reported Captain Dinaux, " everyone was glad to climb into the saddle and ride, but Father Foucauld continued on foot as long as he could, fingering his rosary and reciting litanies. Even over rough or steep terrain he kept up the pace. By five in the morning the sun was already unmercifully hot, the temperature ranging from 100° to 120° in the shade. We all drank 6 to 8 quarts of water a day . . . . But the Padre just kept pushing ahead at his rapid pace. He would only stop when a bad storm blew up, or when someone threatened to get off his own camel and walk beside him.

" When we stopped for a rest, we camped in quadrangle formation, sleeping on the open desert, without benefit of tents, our rifles loaded, the natives in their *burnouses* ready for action .... I always let the Padre have one corner of the quadrangle where he could be more or less to himself and have leisure to pray. Whenever the schedule permitted, he would have himself awakened early by the sergeant of the guard, put up a tent in a flash and say Mass. One of us always assisted at this Mass, and it was an inspiration for all of us to see the extraordinary fervor he put into it. He seemed, actually, to be in ecstasy. "

It was during one of these stops, on June 25, 1905, that the guards sounded an alarm. The whole camp came to life in a hurry, seeing on the horizon, over the vast sea of rocks, a formation of camel-riding troops advancing toward them on a wide front. Who could they be?

Everyone waited a long time with bated breath, until those approaching could be identified. No doubt about it, this was the great Amenokal Moussa, escorted by the elite of his clan, the Ken Rela. What an unforgettable sight — these powerful, stately warriors, peering out from behind their blue veils, astride their sumptuously saddled camels and holding their Touareg weapons in readiness!

They came to a coordinated halt, as precisely executed as though some drillmaster had given the order, although actually no oral command was heard. The Amenokal continued forward alone to meet Captain Dinaux, and exchanged a series of solemn greetings with him. Then the escorts of the two caravans went through a formal meeting ceremony, culminating in the indispensable ritual of a tea party.

This out of the way, the Amenokal declared himself ready to make the proper amends for any difficulties caused by his indecision and to submit unconditionally to the authority of France. From that moment on, the solemnities began to exhibit a more relaxed atmosphere.

The two caravans traveled together for several days, giving Captain Dinaux a chance to acquaint Moussa with Charles de Foucauld, introducing him as " a Christian *marabout* who serves the one God, who loves solitude, and who would like to study the language of the Touareg. He was one who could render a great service to the peoples of the Hoggar, and would make a valuable counselor. "

The discussion lasted for several sessions, and during the series of talks, the idea of Tamanrasset as a residence for Charles was first suggested. " Tamanrasset, " the Amenokal explained, "is where the Dag-Rali have a kind of headquarters, and they are the largest and most loyal of the tribes subject to me. "

Moussa had already sized Charles up on his first encounter with him, and his soul-piercing eyes told him this was a man he could trust. " I'd be willing to bet my life on him, " was Moussa's way of putting it.

Charles, meanwhile, had been sounding out the Amenokal. " A very capable man, " he concluded, " intelligent, very honest, a devout Moslem,

135

benevolent; but at the same time ambitious, a lover of money, pleasures, and honor. "

After 15 days of traveling together, the Amenokal left his new friends to return to his Touareg people. Captain Dinaux escorted Charles toward Tamanrasset. They picked their way through a maze of desert canyons, emerging finally onto a vast plateau. No plant life grew in this region of rocks — no shade of any kind and no breezes blowing. And the sandy bed of the Wadi Tamanrasset, etched through the center of the plateau, was dry most of the year. In the western part were a few wells, some scrawny bushes, a handful of huts inhabited by the Harratins, who scratched out a living by planting barley on little patches of thin soil. This was the village of Tamanrasset, where around 20 families were scattered along the bank of the dry gulch for a distance of about two miles. To the east rose the jagged foothills of the Ahaggar Mountains, dominated in the distance by Ilaman, highest peak of the Sahara.

Here, in all this vast, sun-baked emptiness, in this domain of solitude, on these rocks where the Touareg sometimes pitched their red tents, Charles built himself a hut of reeds just like the Harratin homes.

He also began building a peculiar little stone house, using a mortar of dry mud. It was an incredible piece of work — long, low, and narrow, the walls a yard thick. There were no windows, hardly a peephole in the whole structure; just one little doorway that could only be reached by climbing over a massive embankment two feet high, designed to discourage horned vipers from dropping in for a visit. The flat roof was pieced together from the undressed branches of local shrubs, finished off with reeds and mud. It was shelter against the sun, in other words, but not against a rainstorm. The interior of this tunnel-like building was separated into two compartments — one reserved as a chapel, the other a work area. Each part was nine feet long and about five feet wide.

The reed hut next door was to serve as a kitchen, as a place to entertain guests, and as living quarters for Paul Embarek, if that restless catechumen would finally settle down.

It was not too long before every Harratin farmer and every Touareg nomad on the entire plateau of Tamanrasset had visited the hermitage of the " *marabout* of the red heart " at least once. The hermitage door was always open, and every visitor was received as a brother. " Yes, Laperrine is his friend, " the Touareg would say to themselves, " and he, Laperrine, is a powerful man. But he lives 500 miles from here, while the *marabout,* living alone here in the Hoggar, is one who really trusts us. " And the Touareg had too lively a sense of honor to miss the profound message conveyed by this trust. It was the first time a white man, altogether unarmed, had ever placed himself so completely at their mercy.

This did not mean that at first they had no question marks in their minds about him. " He is a *marabout,* no doubt about it. But he is a Christian, not a Moslem. Why did he leave his own people to come here with us? He gives alms instead of asking for them. Why? Why? Why? "

But with time their questionings became less insistent. Usually one good chat with him would dispel all suspicions. And gradually Charles became their confidant, almost a spiritual director. If faith in Christ proved a wall of separation, at least their common faith in God was a means of uniting them. And when they came to him, he reminded them of the ancient law which was also their common heritage — the law of Sinai, which tells us how to worship God and practice His commandments.

He even reminded the Amenokal of that law, when in October he and his fellow warriors brought their camels to enjoy those few tufts of vegetation that recent rains had brought to the edges of the Tamanrasset plateau. In a very short time the two men had developed a profound friendship — a relationship so intimate that Moussa began to feel in his heart that he had met a real man of God. From that moment on, it was the most logical thing in the world for the supreme ruler of the Hoggar to have Father Foucauld become his guide and teacher. And so, from October 1905 onward, Charles de Foucauld, a Frenchman and a Christian priest, became the lifelong counselor (and virtually the " chaplain ") of a Touareg chieftain who considered himself a devout follower of Mohammed.

In fact when the Amenokal expressed his concerns for the religious laxity that had been growing among his people, Charles de Foucauld recommended to him a reverence for the will of the Most High and a desire to know it as perfectly as possible. " The more you know it, the more you will love it; the more you love it, the more faithfully you will carry it out. " So then, Charles told him, he must pray — pray much, in fact — fast and give alms, strive to practice all the virtues, to combat evildoing, to honor the dignity of labor, to strengthen family life, to train his children in living the good life.

And when Moussa divulged his fears for the survival of his people, always threatened as they were by widespread famine, Charles suggested that if the entire Touareg nation would work together they could develop agriculture and livestock raising throughout their land.

When the Amenokal, with his acute sense of honor, complained to him about certain inconsistencies the French were guilty of and of certain dirty tricks the interpreters had played on the Touareg, Charles counseled him not to reply in kind. " The more you succeed in keeping the peace and working for the good of the Hoggar, the less the French will have cause to interfere in your affairs. " As for translators, he suggested doing without them. Why couldn't the Touareg study French? " Learn French, not in order to be our subjects, but to be our equals; to deal with us face to face without the need of intermediaries, and then sooner or later all the military and public posts in the Hoggar will probably be filled by your own countrymen. "

When it came to Charles' opinions on French colonial policy, he was more than perceptive; he was prophetic: " The French empire of north-western Africa — he wrote in his diary — consolidated by the occupation of Morocco and the union of Algeria with the Sudan, thanks to the conquest of the Saharan regions, will be either the strength or the weakness of France, depending on the wisdom of its administration. Its population of thirty million will, if peace is maintained, double itself in the next fifty years. By then it will have made rapid progress materially, it will be a rich country traversed by railroads, populated by people who can use European weapons of defense, who will be accustomed to European disciplines, and whose intellectuals will be trained in European schools. Unless we know how to make these people a part of us, they will throw us out. Not only will we lose our empire, but the very unity we have forged among them will be turned against us. They will then be hostile, terrifying, barbarian neighbors. "

He was able to distill his whole concept of how colonizers should be related to the colonized into the crystal clearness of a short, simple sentence: " A nation that has colonies is indebted to them in the same way as fathers toward their children —

so to educate and instruct them that they will become equals or superiors. "

Thus Charles spent several years with the Touareg, keeping in constant contact with everyone from the supreme ruler to the poorest family. Meanwhile he was collecting Touareg poetry, prose, and proverbs, and was even writing a Touareg grammar. Every year he went north to Ghardaïa for Confession, to make a retreat, and to take counsel with Monsignor Guérin. Then he would spend a month or so at Beni-Abbès with his old friends, French and Arab, who would visit him at the *khaoua*.

Every once in a while the ever vacillating Paul Embarek would suddenly disappear, leaving him in the lurch. These were always thoroughly unhappy times for Charles, because then he could not offer Mass or adore the Blessed Sacrament. But word finally came from the Holy See, giving him permission to celebrate without a server. It was wonderful news to him.

During the great famine of 1907-8, it did not rain for 17 months. " This means complete starvation, " he wrote, " in a country where milk is the staple food — and the only food for the poor. When the land dries up, so do the goats. And as the goats go, so do the people. "

Once every day Charles gathered all the children of the Tamanrasset plateau around his hut, and fed them until their accumulated hunger

141

was gone. It often happened, Laperrine tells us, that "when he saw all those little ragamuffins enjoying their food, Father Foucauld didn't have the heart to save something for himself."

Charles finally deprived himself of so much of the food he actually needed, that he became seriously ill. "I have no cough," he wrote his sister, "and no pain in my chest, but the least movement makes me gasp for air, and I feel like fainting. A day or two ago I thought it was all over for me." When Laperrine learned of his desperate condition, he arranged to send him the medicine he thought would be most useful at the moment, a shipment of food.

It was at about the same time that Charles received word of his special dispensation granted by the Holy See. This he welcomed as even better medicine, because he yearned not so much for earthly bread, as for the bread of the Eucharist.

He had felt very close to death in 1908. If he had died, what would have happened to his ideal? Never once had anyone responded to his repeated requests for followers to share his life.

When at last the first autumn rain broke the drought, he left for France on a new assignment: to find, at any cost, someone who would join his projected Union of the Brothers and Sisters of the Sacred Heart of Jesus, a kind of Third Order to which he could entrust his spiritual patrimony hoping that someday or other someone would arise to carry on his work. On this occasion he gained the cooperation of his cousin Marie de Bondy, his sister Marie de Blic, and a few others. He made subsequent trips to France, always for the same purpose, but at his death all that survived was a prayer group of maybe 50 persons that had been organized by this Union.

All the loneliness in which he was forced to live his " life of Nazareth " weighed heavily on his heart. Then finally one day it seemed as though his high hopes were about to be realized. From Monsignor Guérin, at Ghardaïa, he learned that Brother Michael, a young man from Brittany who had served as a Zouave and was now a lay brother with the White Fathers, had asked to become his disciple. Charles took him along at once to Beni-Abbès, But here the severe life of self-denial at the " *khaoua* of the Sacred Heart " began at once to undermine the neophyte's health.

After a few months they left for the Hoggar, but had to make a rest stop at In Salah, for Brother Michael's sake. It turned out to be more than a " rest " for the poor disciple, who had to stay in bed for extensive treatment. The Medical Corps gave him a " no go. " If he continued on to the Hoggar, he would die on the way.

And so, on the one occasion when someone might have gone to the desert with Charles to be his associate and the first of the Little Brothers, Charles ended up completing the journey alone.

In 1910 there was another severe drought. The Touareg frantically climbed the most impenetrable ravines of their mountains to find a little pasture. The Tamanrasset plateau was deserted, except for the Harratins. Charles reacted to this with the decision to build a hermitage at the top of Mt. Asekrem, about 8,800 feet above sea level, where the Touareg were encamped.

It was four days' travel through the rocky floors of steep ravines, hemmed in by gigantic cliffs of black, blue, and red rock, to reach the base of a 300 foot stone wall, whose flat summit could be reached only by climbing straight up its face. At the top was a magnificently barren plateau covered with green boulders, tormented day and night by the whistling and howling of insistent winds. Here where all the fantastic peaks of the Hoggar passed in a ragged but ravishing review before him, Charles built his new hermitage: a chapel and a small workroom.

" I am absolutely alone up here, on Asekrem, and the view is out of this world; it is the weirdest collection of peaks, pyramids, and piled rocks I have ever seen. "

But the most welcome sight for him, during all the months he remained there, was on the slopes below him, which became covered with sweet-smelling vegetation whenever there were even a few drops of rain. Here, then, the Touareg pitched their long, low, red-leather tents, next to their grazing flocks, in order to enjoy the good mountain milk. And every day some of the Touareg made the long climb to his hermitage and then returned to their tents, making much the same comment as one of their high-caste women had made in 1907, when Charles had saved her five children from starvation: " It is horrible to think that such a good man as he will go to hell when he dies because he is not a Moslem. " And they prayed to Allah for the Christian *marabout*, committing themselves to greater respect for God's will according to the laws of Sinai as a direct result of Charles' teaching.

Ba Hamou, Moussa's secretary, eventually came to live with him on Asekrem. He was a " loan " from the Amenokal, as a sign of that nobleman's friendship. Moussa knew that a few month's companionship of this kind would be very useful to Charles, because Ba Hamou was a walking encyclopedia of ethnographic and linguistic knowledge, and Charles was glad to get his help in his preparation of a Touareg-French dictionary.

But when winter began to arrive, blowing its icy gusts across the flat summit of Asekrem, Ba Hamou complained that he had quite enough " vacation " to suit him. There was nothing for Father Foucauld to do but return to Tamanrasset and to the long, narrow hermitage that General Laperrine had christened " The Frigate " because it resembled a trim warship in that rough ocean of rocks.

At Tamanrasset, Brother Charles continued to receive every Touareg who came to pasture his goats on the plateau. By now it was an established custom of these people to stop in for a cup of tea with him every time they were in the vicinity. They shared their bread and milk and cheese with him, just as he had shared their suffering with them during the long hunger of the dry spells. They spontaneously demonstrated their deep affection for him. And they entered into many a lengthy discussion, telling him mainly about their practical affairs or problems. But as time went on they turned more and more to personal questions: " What are you writing about? What are those little pictures you're drawing? "

Then Charles would explain what the sacred symbols meant, and read for them his translation of some portion of the Gospel, especially the parables. And the asceticism he practiced had a way of disarming their defenses, a little more each time.

But the hospitable hermit of the Hoggar, he who was a brother to the nomad, he who sought to be the lowliest of servants and to serve the world's most forsaken people, was sometimes catapulted suddenly into national affairs, serving as arbiter in decisions and disputes involving the Hoggar and the French government. A case in point was the time General Laperrine decided to make a sizable shipment of material to Temassinine, on the Tripolitanian border, where the construction of Fort Flatters had only just been completed.

Such an expedition, through uncivilized, untracked territory, called for the use of almost all the camels of the Hoggar, plus the hiring of several hundred men whose living expenses had to be paid for several months. So Laperrine used Brother Charles as a go-between in asking the Amenokal for camels and personnel. On the strength of this intercession the Amenokal not only granted both requests but even consented to lead the great caravan himself.

For his part of the bargain, however, Moussa asked through his intermediary that the Touareg " Meharists " be paid in advance, so that when they got to Temassinine they would have the money to shop with. And Laperrine, since his friend Foucauld stood behind the contract, agreed to such terms. But when payday came, there were some Frenchmen who seemed ready to overlook part of the wages agreed to. Then Charles made energetic protests until the " Meharists " received every penny they had coming to them.

When Amenokal Moussa assumed command of the vast convoy, he left his homeland temporarily in charge of a trusted lieutenant, Akmed Ag Echecherif. Laperrine also assured Charles that his own French lieutenant, Sigonney, would keep close watch over the Hoggar during the three months or so when the territory would be inhabited only by old people, women, and children.

The person who actually governed the Amenokal's domain in his absence was a woman of extraordinary abilities. " The one who makes the real decisions," Charles wrote at the time, " is Dacine.... She rules without seeming to rule, and Akmed Ag Echecherif is only her chief executive. She is very intelligent and is well informed on all that is going on. He is energetic and a man of good will. Both of them are devout Moslems. One could not ask for a better setup."

Every warrior of the Hoggar was in love with Dacine, a beautiful, spiritually minded woman who wrote charming poetry. The Amenokal himself was one of her most ardent admirers, as evidenced by a love poem he had dedicated to her:

> " Dacine is the moon;
> more thrilling her head and shoulders
> than the mane of a colt
> cavorting in the April fields of grain.
> God has made her beautiful and graceful.
> All reverence her,
> yes, all love her.
> It is impossible for any woman to marry
> as long as Dacine is free.
> Yes, she is free, she is graceful;
> she can play the one-stringed flute
> and sing with great skill.... "

But Dacine, although affectionately fond of the Amenokal, had not accepted his amorous advances.

> " Freely would I give all my people
> and all the flocks on my mountains
> as well as the rich meadows
> that make the goats

and the camels fecund —
from Gougueran to here,
and as far as Bornou,
from Arar to Afeston —
if only you reigned in my heart
as the sun among the stars . . . .
But, she, alas,
returns my loving glance no more
nor courts my tenderness . . . . "

A hundred other warriors' voices echoed the Amenokal's love for Dacine. But among those hundred warriors she had chosen a certain Afelan. Still this did not destroy the friendship of Moussa. Instead, whenever officially he left his affairs in the hands of this or that lieutenant, he was actually entrusting the defense of the Hoggar to this exceptional young woman.

Charles thought of her as " intelligent and well-informed. " Dacine, for her part, knew of Charles' friendship for Moussa and that Moussa returned that sentiment to the point of asking his advice. She approved of it, in fact. And as long as Brother Charles of Jesus lived in the Sahara, this young poetess who devoutly worshiped Allah was one of his closest allies.

The Great War began in 1914, and Charles got word of it about a month after it erupted. The first reverberations, in fact, were heard rumbling here in the heart of Africa. From Algiers he learned that the Moroccan guerrillas had stepped up their attacks all along the border. In Tripolitania

149

all hell had broken loose. And the oasis of Cufra, in Cyrenaica, headquarters of the great Senusite sect of Moslems, had given birth to a revolutionary ferment that was beginning to cause disquiet even among the Touareg of the Hoggar.

At his hermitage, Charles de Foucauld was showing signs of deterioration. Malnutrition, scurvy, fever, and difficulty in breathing, were all afflicting him. But his rule of life was still the very words his mother pronounced on her deathbed, at Strasbourg and which he had sought to live ever since his conversion: " Lord, not my will, but thine be done. "

The French were feeling ill-at-ease about his living all alone at Tamanrasset in his unprotected hermitage, when at any moment a wave of Senusite fanaticism could sweep everything away. Orders were sent to Charles to withdraw to Fort Motylinski, 30 miles to the east.

He refused, unconditionally, to move. How could he abandon the plateau where his beloved Harratins lived and where the Touareg knew they could always find him?

If he was under orders to get inside some fortification, then he would build his own stockade, right there at Tamanrasset, where the Harratins and the Touareg could find refuge also, in case there was any trouble.

So his friends all pitched in to help him build such a fort. The French supplied it with munitions, and he left the hermitage for the new stockade, taking along his altar, chalice, ciborium, monstrance, vestments, and manuscripts.

He would live the life of Nazareth in the fortress as he had lived in the hermitage.

And so the evening of December 1, 1916, arrived, and as the shadows stole out of the canyons of the Hoggar and climbed up toward the towers of his Tamanrasset fortress, that fatal knock sounded at the gate.

" Who's there? "

" It's the mail, " said the familiar voice of his Harratin friend El Madani.

Charles opened the door, and rough hands — ten, twenty, sixty of them — reached out of the dark, grabbed him, threw him to his knees, tied his wrists and ankles together behind his back, then bound his entire body with ropes.

He could see the dark outlines of about thirty Senusites around him, along the edge of the moat that circled the walls outside. They were mostly from the tribe of Ajjer, and they had crept in through the Hoggar ravines without being discovered. Then Charles saw some other men arriving with Paul Embarek, whom they had taken by surprise in his hut. So Paul was also a prisoner. But Charles noticed that he was not tied up.

For half an hour — or was it an eternity? — he watched them enter and re-enter the stokade, robbing it of all its weapons and religious articles and smashing everything they could not carry away.

151

Everyone participated in the plundering except one Senusite who looked like an overgrown boy. He stood just two paces from Charles without moving. " Keep an eye on him, Sermi ag Thora! " the others instructed him, and the young man never let his eyes — or the business end of his rifle — wander away from the prisoner.

" I must expect to die a martyr, destitute, stretched upon the ground... disfigured... covered with blood... the victim of a violent death. " Do you remember when he wrote those words? Or these: " Let me live each moment as though I were to die tonight, as a martyr.... Let me prepare unceasingly for that martyrdom and accept it without lifting a finger in self-defense, like the Lamb of God. "

Suddenly the alarm was sounded. In the moment of silence that followed, Charles heard the hoofbeats of camels. The two Meharists, not suspecting what had happened, were coming for the mail.

The Senusites thought they were being attacked and threw themselves upon the unknown challengers, screaming and firing their weapons wildly. Sermi ag Thora, the overgrown boy, lost his head. Charles may have made some movement that gave the impression he was trying to escape. Or the boy may simply have been so frightened that he did not realize what he was doing. At any rate, he pulled the trigger, and in spite of his fear, his aim was good.

The bound body of Charles de Foucauld, little brother of Jesus, went slowly limp. The bullet had gone through his head from the right ear to the left eye and lodged in the red brick wall of the fortress, to the left of the doorway.

The Little Brothers that Charles Never Knew

You may wonder what happened after that. When the Senusites had assassinated Charles de Foucauld as well as the two Meharists who had come to get his mail, the others spent nearly the entire night feasting on the slaughtered camel of the Meharist, Bou Aïcha. Then they went into the fortress to get some rest.

But as the morning of December 2nd was dawning, the sentinel on duty saw a shadow approaching among the distant rock heaps of Tamanrasset. It was a camel rider! He sounded the alarm, and the Senusites posted themselves at the gun ports on the wall and in the ditch outside of it. When the dark figure drew closer, a command was given to fire, and the Meharist toppled over onto the jagged rocks. It was Kouider ben Lakhal, a courier from Fort Motylinski, bringing the mail for Father Foucauld.

The Saharan sun was in full command of the Tamanrasset landscape when the Senusites broke camp, leading their booty-laden camels over the hilly Hoggar terrain, in the direction of Tripolitania.

Shortly afterward Paul Embarek, who had been fortunate enough to escape the general massacre, arrived with some of the Harratin villagers. It was a chilling sight that greeted their eyes.

Tearfully they gathered up the remains of Charles de Foucauld, still wearing the bonds in which he died, his back and knees bent double, his wrists still tied to his ankles. They lowered him reverently into the ditch beneath the fortress walls, laid beside him the bodies of the three Meharists — Bou Aïcha, Boudjema ben Brahim, Kouider ben Lakhal — and covered all four corpses with rocks.

Then Paul Embarek, accompanied by a Harratin, rushed to Fort Motylinski across 30 miles of open desert, arriving before nightfall. There they informed Captain de la Roche of the tragedy.

The bugle sounded a general alarm, and the Captain and his men raced after the Senusites. For two weeks they searched every grotesque nook and cranny of the Hoggar labyrinth.

When they found their quarry on the 17th of December, command was given to " fire at will, " and this command was to be repeated for several days. A few of the Senusites were shot down, but most of them left the fray and escaped.

On December 21st, Captain de la Roche returned to Tamanrasset, arrayed his men along the edge of the ditch in front of the fortress, and gave the order to present arms. Then he planted a cross among the stones that served as burial ground for the four slain men.

After that he entered the fort, where he found everything as topsy turvy as the aftermath of a tornado. The wooden crucifix had been ground underfoot into the sand, in the courtyard books were torn to ribbons, manuscripts had been torn, soiled, scattered all over the place. The little wooden " Stations of the Cross, " which Foucauld himself had etched with a pen, had been thrown down and now lay among the rubble of shattered furniture, garbage, and doors torn from their hinges.

The Captain went back outside, his eyes cast to the ground and a lump in his throat. Suddenly he saw the glint of a bright object lying in a little pocket of sand among the gray rocks, and stooped down to pick it up. It was the little monstrance that had belonged to Charles de Foucauld, containing a consecrated Host.

The Captain's hands trembled noticeably. He cleaned the sand off the monstrance, wrapped it in a little piece of cloth, slipped it into the inside pocket of his jacket, and took it back to Fort Motylinski.

Back at the fort, Captain de la Roche kept remembering something Charles had once told him: " If anything should happen to me, please take the monstrance with the Blessed Sacrament to Ghardaïa and turn it over to the White Fathers. "

With the political situation in the Hoggar, aggravated by Senusite infiltrations, becoming more alarming every day, the Captain could not conscientiously leave his post long enough to travel so far north, and he did not want to entrust anyone else with the monstrance.

Should he take Communion all by himself? He had heard of such situations occuring before, but he could not bring himself to take such a step. Finally he shared the problem with one of his best and most upright junior officers. They went together out into the majesty of the desert, a little distance from the fort, under the bright vault of the sky, and in the presence of God, De la Roche removed his white gloves, took the monstrance from his pocket, unwrapped it, and opened it. Then the junior officer knelt in front of him, took out the Sacred Host and consumed it.

When news of the slaughter at Tamanrasset traveled via desert grapevine — the Touareg caravans that traversed the rocky Hoggar desert — to the red tent of Moussa, the Amenokal broke into a desperate, uninhibited cry of grief. Then he sat down on his little rug and wrote to Marie de Blic. In his letter he proposed the most unimaginably savage means of revenge — thoughts that his slain friend would have gently rebuked. But he also expressed, in the name of his people, what the sacrifice of Charles de Foucauld had most truly and deeply meant to them: " Praise to the one God! To our noble friend Marie, sister of Charles our *marabout,* whom those treacherous people of

Ajjer have assassinated.... From the moment I received word of the death of our friend and your brother, my eyes have been closed with grief, and all is darkness around me. My tears run freely and I am in great distress. His death has left me a broken man. The place where those treacherous schemers killed him is some distance from here, for he was killed in the Hoggar but I am now in the Adrar. But, please God, those who have killed our *marabout* we will eventually overtake, and they will feel the full weight of our revenge. Give greetings in my name to your children, your husband, and your friends, and tell them that the *marabout* Charles has not just died for you, but for us all. May God show mercy upon him, and may we all meet together in Paradise. "

He has died for us all! Thus the martyrdom of Charles de Foucauld assumed sublime importance to the people of the Hoggar, as their Amenokal has so clearly documented for us.

But you are still wondering what happened after that. Ten years went by, and in 1927 an investigation began for the cause of beatification of Charles de Foucauld. His body was transferred to a grave in El Goléa, but no living testimony of his " ideal of Nazareth " could be found anywhere in the Sahara.

It was another six years before René Voillaume initiated (in 1933) the first small group known as the Little Brothers of Jesus. Charles de Foucauld was recognized as their founder, and Voillaume was named as his successor.

In 1939 the Little Sisters of Jesus became a reality, although in 1933 a female congregation known as the Little Sisters of the Sacred Heart had already espoused the ideal of Foucauld. But the rule of this earlier group called for a greater emphasis on contemplation.

Thus the blood spilled among the rocks of Tamanrasset had germinated three little sprouts in a little over 20 years. In the present book we will say something about the two groups that have developed more closely according to the ideal of Nazareth as Charles de Foucauld had originally conceived it, lived it, and explained it in his various written versions of the rule.

There was only a handful to begin with, but today their Fraternities have spread across all five continents. There are now over 400 Little Brothers, and the Little Sisters are over 800. And their novitiates are not suffering from any dearth of vocations.

They live in groups of three, four, or five, called Fraternities. Among the working class of the great population centers, they have become as workers. Among the nomads of the great deserts they have become as nomads, living in their houses and tents and doing manual labor.

Says a *Ruhr-Bild* release: " A while ago we came across two photographs that seemed very inconsistent with each other at the time. The first pictured the little stone hermitage built in 1910 by Charles de Foucauld on the world's most isolated location, the wind-swept summit of Asekrem, surrounded by the ferocious peaks of the Hoggar in Sahara's deep south.

" The other picture showed the Roubaix Fraternity, situated on an uninviting blind alley. It can be entered only from the inner court of an enormous row of tenements filled to overflowing with mineworkers and their families. The bicycles of three Little Brothers stand outside, black with coal dust. Inside, apparently, there was scarcely enough room to turn around....

" Were the two pictures really contradictory? Not at all. These Little Brothers of Jesus who work in the mine pits of Roubaix and live in their off-hours in this human anthill, are being completely faithful, in the 1960's, to the life led by Brother Charles in the first two decades of this century. Theirs is one and the same testimony. "

When it comes to possessions, the Little Brothers own absolutely nothing, not even the little places they live in. They are always rented from someone. Depending on the latitude and longitude, their " apartment " could be some shack in a shanty town, a bamboo hut, a cave, a gypsy-style house-on-wheels, a nomad's tent, or a couple of rooms in some cheap tenement of a metropolitan area. Be it a barracks, a hut, a cave, a wagon, a tent, or an apartment, it exhibits the same poverty to anyone who enters: a table, some benches, a

couple of chairs, a few books, some folding beds . . . .
Everything expresses the same motif of simplicity,
the same manner of living. Even the air one
breathes in such a place seems to convey a sense
of poverty loved for its own sake, a witness and
testimony to the occupants' spiritual detachment
from the world.

" Manual labor, " wrote Charles when he was
Trappist Brother Marie-Alberic of Our Lady of the
Sacred Heart community in Syria, " is more burdensome than anyone might imagine who has not
performed it . . . . What compassion it gives you for
the poor, what love for the laboring man! At last
one can know the worth of a piece of bread, when
he has known from experience how much work is
required to produce it. One learns to have pity on
the man who works for a living, after he has
shared his toil. "

And each Little Brother of Jesus literally earns
his bread " by the sweat of his brow. " Only during
his novitiate and the period of study that follows it,
will he be subsidized in any way. Once his studies
are completed and he has pronounced his final
vows, he will belong heart and soul to the laboring
class, with all the consequences this entails.

The Little Brothers take their turn, along with
everyone else, at the various work shifts, they
receive the same low pay, they participate in
strikes, they face the same working hazards, the
same occupational illnesses — because they have
given their assent to this from the very beginning
of their novitiate.

If some business or industry comes to realize that these are professed religious (a fact they do not try to conceal) there may be an attempt to extend certain privileges to them. But the Little Brothers always refuse such special treatment, anything that would detract them from attaining their ideal, the " last place " of Charles de Foucauld. They have vowed always to seek this last place both in their positions of employment and in the choice of a place to live, in line with Brother Charles' first rule, formulated in 1896, which called for living " among the very poorest of people " and " dedicated principally to the most disinherited and most forsaken of people. "

But there is a very special way in which the Little Brothers are dedicated to the disinherited and forsaken. Charles de Foucauld had as his spirit and ideal the hidden life of Jesus that He lived until thirty years of age. Thus a memorandum issued by Prior René Voillaume in 1938 absolutely forbade the Fraternities from participating in any sort of apostolic activity. They are not to engage in parish activities, nor is their private chapel to be used for parish services. Even when they are off work and they retire to the enclosure of their Fraternity, they must excuse themselves from activities promoting the conversion of unbelievers, religious education, the care of orphans, schoolteaching, or any other activity inconsistent with their hidden life of silence and prayer.

The Little Brothers maintain normal social contacts with their neighbors and working companions without resorting to any special devices to effect their conversion to the faith.

" All things to all men " is a motto that the Little Brothers seek to carry out literally. The door of the Fraternity is open always to everyone, day or night, as it was with the khaoua of the Sacred Heart at Beni-Abbès, the hermitage at Tamanrasset, or the stone hut on Mt. Asekrem.

In every Fraternity, whether in Belgium or Lebanon, in Spain or the Congo, the Little Brothers of every race and nationality testify to the supranational character of Christian love. They receive everyone who knocks at the door — to ask advice, a piece of bread, or a bit of friendship. Thus they are willing to identify with the poor in every particular, to speak the language of their neighbors, to eat the local diet, to celebrate Mass (those who are priests) according to the rite most adapted to their place of residence, and to wear the everyday costume of their fellow workers except during divine services, when they wear a simple gray robe. In a Molsem country, for instance, they speak Arabic, celebrate Mass according to the Melkite rite, and wear the *burnous*. Thus nowhere do they operate as foreigners, nor do they play the role of a missionary or worker-priest. They are religious in the garb of laymen. They live a twentieth-century kind of poverty, just as the monks of earlier times lived a life of poverty suited to their age.

What is new about the testimony of the Little Brothers, something that marks it off from any method of evangelization previously used in the Church, is, as Robert Barrot describes it, " the absolutely disinterested quality " of their presence among the poor. Their simple aim is to be " unprofitable servants " (Luke 17: 10) — in other words mere instruments in God's hands. Thus some soul, if God wills it, will be touched by the testimony of the Gospel lived out in their lives. Sometimes someone will come, not to ask advice or for something to eat, or even for friendship, but to inquire into the reasons for their faith and their hope. The Little Brothers will then answer, and the consequences will be according to God's will. But they do not seek such conversation in any way; they do not provoke these questions, or answer in such a way as to high-pressure the questioner. This is because the Little Brothers have decided to be no more than mute witnesses — even at times misunderstood witnesses — of God's love among men.

The results are rather paradoxical. The more the Brothers seek to be inactive in such work, the more people flock to their Fraternity. The common laborers in the factories where they work have this to say: " At last there are monks who live as we do and as Jesus would live today. "

Yet it doesn't always work that way. There are times, especially in the big population centers, when their mute testimony passes unobserved, seemingly swallowed up in the religious vacuum of their environment. Sometimes, unfortunately, they receive sensational coverage from certain newspapers and magazines noted for their juicy scandal stories.

It is best when they are ignored, when the Little Brothers pass unobserved. Then, at their places of work, perhaps all the dialogue that ever develops is from a matter-of-fact question: " What's that? A badge of some kind? " (The questioner is referring to the red cross and heart that a Little Brother wears on the lapel of his jacket.)

" Yes, it's the symbol of a Catholic religious Order. "

" Not bad. Did you design it yourself? " And that's as far as the conversation gets. Or else they are met with indifference. There is no hostility, no poking of fun. Everyone just keeps a respectful distance.

At the end of a day's work the Little Brothers return to their Fraternity, which is their life-giving cell, above all, because there is a room there reserved as a chapel where they can celebrate Mass in the morning or evening. And every day, even when they are dead tired from their work, they kneel before the Blessed Sacrament for the hours of adoration that their rule prescribes for them daily.

It is certainly no easy job to maintain a life of prayer under the difficult conditions imposed by a life of manual labor, aggravated by the discomfort of cheap, substandard lodging in the midst of the world's most underprivileged human beings. Here is a grueling asceticism that requires one to rise at the crack of dawn each day in order to say Mass before rushing to get to work on time; that continues its demands all day long as the Little Brother lives a life of generous openness toward his fellow workers and then goes home to face neighbors who call on him, and other guests who might come from almost anywhere. From morn till night, and often even in the middle of the night, moment by moment, until death, his soul must be kept in readiness to watch and pray.

One can see that such a life, lived in the spirit of Charles de Foucauld, would require a long and intensive training period, especially since novices must be prepared to make themselves at home in any substandard environment of the world.

After a two-year probationary period spent in a working Fraternity to acquaint the applicant at once and in depth with the strenuous work and difficulties that will be a part of the life to which he aspires, he will begin his novitiate in either France or Spain. At the close of this period he will take his first temporary vows, which will have to be renewed several times during the succeeding years before he takes perpetual vows. The novice is then assigned to a second fraternity for a while, after which he can begin his studies, lasting from three to six years, which will be given him at St. Maximin, near Toulouse. Here he will receive a complete theological, philosophical, and cultural education, which includes training in Hindu mysticism, Moslem theology, Marxist ideology, and Eastern Orthodox Church doctrine, to mention only a sampling of the subjects studied.

After formal studies are completed, the young man must spend quite a bit of time in the heart of the desert, where the soul can more perfectly meditate on the immensity of God and the smallness of one's own self. After this experience he will at last be sent to some location where he begins his career of silence, testifying to God by his presence, by his life of labor and prayer.

Every year new Fraternities of the Little Brothers open in countries where they have not existed before. They work among miners in Belgium, sailors in Brittany, shipyard workers in Hamburg, nomads in the desert, and as voluntary inmates in certain prisons.

The Little Sisters have their international novitiate in Rome, attended by about sixty novices at the present time. They work in a number of countries as nurse aides, as factory personnel, as housekeepers by the day, and as attendants to Bedouin women in the desert.

When you leave Rome by the Via Prenestina, at the city limits you can see the modern beehive-style apartment buildings give way to poor dwellings. On the left-hand side of the road, a hill rises, covered with an untidy undergrowth and some run-down houses. Some streets climb up through this shantytown, their names too dignified to sound appropriate, their pavements full of pot-holes. On up the hill they pass among some dirty red shacks, audaciously referred to as " low-priced housing, " lined up in rows like barracks in a concentration camp. They are actually like basement houses — with roofs, sloping from front to back, that almost reach the ground. There are a few snack shops, a rancid delicatessen, and above one moldy door there is a sign announcing the presence of the Rent Payments Office. The further you go, the more the asphalt on the road begins to disappear, and the " building code " goes completely berserk. You have entered the " kasbah. "

The shacks here are huddled up against each other, equipped with only a few square feet of muddy yard fenced off with chicken wire. They are a mushroom growth of homes, put up almost overnight, because the local authorities cannot order them destroyed unless they were discovered before the roof was put on. Alleyways of clay, eroded by the rains, cluttered with filth, stones, and weeds; heavily patched and mended laundry flapping on the clotheslines; the stripped skeletons of motor scooters left to rust along the banks of miry ditches. Children and chickens seem to be constantly underfoot, and one sees stray dogs, women with saddened eyes, men with fatigued faces, Communist party posters clinging to the walls.

On a street typical of those just described (eight feet in width, more or less) there is a little red house with the same muddy yard a few feet square, fenced off with chicken wire, its wash hung out like all the rest, its windows about the size of a ticket window in some small-town railroad station. It adjoins another house inhabited by a worker's family, but nailed to the left side of the double doorway is a slab of wood bearing the words, written in ink, " Fraternity of Jesus. "

Here live the Little Sisters. You will find two little rooms whitewashed and tinted. It is furnished with the essentials, all very rough in design. There are two photographs of Charles de Foucauld, and on one wall a world map. There is also an unpainted plaster image of the Boy Jesus, as a reminder to the inmates of their " life of Nazareth. " It seems to say: " Don't forget how *little you are!* "

Go through one door and you are in the chapel, a room constructed just like the others, dimensions about 8' by 10', perhaps smaller. But here you can breathe the breezes of paradise. Against the wall facing you, as you enter, is a wooden altar covered with a simple white cloth, and on the altar the Blessed Sacrament is exposed in the plainest monstrance you ever saw. The tabernacle is of copper, some of that good old domestic kind like the pots and pans in grandma's kitchen. There are oil lights and two candles burning, while overhead hangs a wooden cross, the Crucified Figure depicted in a style that is unmistakably that of Charles de Foucauld's sketches.

In each of the two corners flanking the altar there is a little wooden stand. The one on the left holds an inexpensive edition of the Holy Scriptures. The one on the right supports an unglazed terracotta Madonna with Child. Along the walls are hung little unpainted wooden plaques representing the Stations of the Cross. The only markings on each one are a cross perhaps drawn with a pen, and, beneath it, a roman numeral.

On the floor in front of the altar is spread a little coco mat, and two Little Sisters are kneeling there in prayer. They sing the *Veni Creator,* they recite the *Angelus* (for twilight is turning to darkness outside), and they chant the *Tantum Ergo.* Then the little copper door, crudely engraved with the heart-and-cross motif, is made to slide in front of the monstrance. The two candles are extinguished, but the lamps burn on, their light reflected in the Little Sister's eyes.

The religious garb of the Little Sisters is a blue-gray dress that looks like a cross between a nun's habit and a cleaning woman's uniform. A maroon version of the Foucauld heart-and-cross emblem appears on the front of the habit, and they wear a large rosary of wooden beads around the waist. The kerchief on their heads looks for all the world like that of an Italian peasant woman, and is colored blue, like the blue veils of the Touareg people in the Hoggar. And the Little Sisters, instead of merely kneeling before the altar, prostrate themselves in the manner of Moslems at prayer in their ample *burnouses* pressing their foreheads against the ground.

" The Rome Fraternity has three Little Sisters at the moment, " the neighbors told us the day we went to visit them in that incredibly wretched labyrinth of dirty alleys, " and two of them have been here quite a while. " One of them works in a hosiery factory, the other does house-keeping by the day for a private family. The third has just come from Kenya, where she lived among the native Africans. When someone arrives like this, it usually signifies that one of the " veterans " is about to leave. One of the Little Sisters is, in fact, preparing to leave as this is being written. Before coming to Rome, she had been working with a band of gypsies in France. Her next stop is Naples.

For the Little Sisters, as much as for their male counterparts, " transfers " — the most unexpected — are the order of the day, and cause very little anxiety. They pack a suitcase with a few clothes, and away they go! After all, one corner of the world is as good as another. There are poor people, lost people, everywhere they go, ready to show them ever more lowly paths of self-denial and abnegation that will guide their feet into that " lowest place " that Jesus attained by His sacrifice on the cross.

Wherever they go, the Little Brothers of Jesus adapt their way of life to the environment in which they are called to live, even incorporating local culture motifs into the chapels they design. Thus at the Fraternity in Charleroi, Belgium, the altar in the chapels is supported by a scaffolding just like the one used in the local mine shafts. At Concarneau, a French fishing village famous for its sardines, fishing nets are used to decorate the walls. In Lebanon, Iraq, and Pakistan, a square altar is used, ornamented with drapery, with the addition of icons arranged according to local custom. At Hamburg-Altona, a German seaport, the present Fraternity chapel was once the site of a coal deposit. It is only about 70 square feet, this little house of God occupying the basement beneath a barber shop. The barber is their landlord, in fact.

At first glance it might seem that they are thrown out into danger, at the mercy of the world, in this or that haunt of misery, left to their own devices. Nothing could be more untrue. A great bond of unity is always maintained among the Little Brothers, and there is a continual exchange of news. In every Fraternity someone is responsible to the Prior of the Order and must correspond with him every two or three months. The letters are always simple and intimate, recording recent happenings: experiences, difficult moments, joys and sorrows. These "diaries" are then put in printed form and circulated among the Fraternities, so that everyone keeps in touch with what the others are doing. Thus the Little Brothers, while appearing isolated among the Andean Cordilleras or the restless Congo jungles, are actually never out of touch with one another.

If the obscurity that regulates every moment of their common life and the very personal nature of their correspondence did not preclude the collection and general publication of these letter-diaries, the world would have a very important document at its disposal, independent of any political viewpoint. It would be the most formidable scientific text written on the material and spiritual misery afflicting our generation.

With all due respect for the intimate nature of such letters, we quote here from the closing lines of one Brother's description of the social situation in which he has been working: " We ask all Little Brothers to bear a part of the burden of prayer for these matters, because we here cannot adequately do so by ourselves. The lack of unity between the people around us and ourselves is entirely too great. Pray for W., a fellow worker of mine at the factory, who worked 76 hours this week — just for the money in it! Pray for G., who does not get along with his wife. One of their big problems is that they and their child have had only one room to live in for the last five years. Pray for H., 21 years old, who does janitorial work at the shopping center. His companions are always making fun of him because he stutters. Pray for all those the Lord has entrusted to us, and for all those whose salvation is hindered because of our lack of love. "

Heart-rending appeals like this pour in from everywhere: from North Africa, where the Brothers work among Arabs and the European proletariat, to the Cameroons and Iran, where they are among lepers; from the Fraternities scattered through the Moslem world or in Buddhist Ceylon to those in the metropolitan slums of Peru, Vietnam, Japan, Belgium, Germany, and England: from the Fraternities that testify to the life of Nazareth among the aborigines of Venezuela and Angola, to those who work in agriculture and brave the high seas to be among the fishing folk.

From all these places there is the same flow of news and the same requests for prayer, because in accordance, with Father René Voillaume's directions, the Little Brothers work " among all those who must earn their living in an atmosphere of hopeless isolation, and those whose only goal in life is materialism. "

In accordance with Voillaume's request, the Little Brothers continue to be, everywhere they go, those who differ from others in that their real nourishment is their faith: a faith that allows them to be " brothers " to everyone. " This interior life, this life of faith, " says Foucauld's successor, " is what enables our poor testimony to be heard — maybe a few spoken words, an answer given in friendship, a word of advice nearly drowned in the roar of a machine. This voice of the individual in the midst of these masses will find its echo among the multitudes, will have repercussions in the Church of Silence behind the Iron Curtain, can reach even to the remotest outposts of the Marxist empire ... because Jesus is Lord even of the impossible. "